THE KINDS OF MANKIND

THE KINDS

OF MANKIND

An Introduction to Race and Racism

by MORTON KLASS and HAL HELLMAN

Illustrated with drawings by Visa-Direction, Inc., and with photographs

J. B. LIPPINCOTT COMPANY   Philadelphia / New York / Toronto

for SHEILA [2]

Acknowledgment:

The authors gratefully acknowledge
the advice and assistance
of Paula G. Rubel and Abraham Rosman,
of the Anthropology Department
at Barnard College,
Columbia University.

Contents

Foreword

When the Cherokee Indians first came into contact with Europeans and Africans, they were astonished at how different in appearance human beings could be. They wondered about these differences —and it wasn't long before a myth came into existence to explain them.

When the time came to make man, the myth begins, the Creator built an oven. Then he molded three figures, much like gingerbread men, out of dough. But the Creator had no previous experience in making men, and had no idea how long the dough figures had to bake. The first one he took out too soon; it was underdone. Pale and unpleasant in color, "half-baked" if you will, this was the ancestor of the white man.

The Creator waited a bit, then removed the second figure from the oven. This one was just right—light brown and pleasing to the eye of the Creator. From this figure all Indians are said to descend.

So pleased was the Creator with his second effort that he forgot to watch the oven, and when he finally pulled the third figure out it was too late. From this scorched and blackened figure, say the Cherokees, all black men are descended.

We may smile and shrug our shoulders at the Cherokee attempt to explain the differences they saw among human groups. And yet, we too wonder about these differences. Indeed all men have wondered, probably since that distant time when man first developed the capacity to wonder, why strangers should look—and act—so different from one's own friends and neighbors.

When human beings are puzzled about something their reaction is the same throughout the world: they search for an explanation that will satisfy them. All people require explanations that fit the facts they know. In recent centuries, scientists have been more exacting in their search for both facts and explanations.

With all this curiosity about human variation, with all this search for explanation by both the ordinary thoughtful person and the trained scientist, one might expect that the problem of human differences would have long since been solved to everyone's satisfaction. There are, however, many questions still unanswered. Even more surprising is that much of what scholars *have* learned is misunderstood by many people.

"There are no differences; all people are the same," some of your friends may insist. "Not so," say others, "there are basic differences between races of humans. Not only that, but these differences are such that certain races are, and will forever remain, superior to others!" Some will argue that all differences are merely skin-deep—and are countered by those who claim that an expert can examine a piece of human bone and announce with certainty whether its owner was a European, Asian or African.

Such confusion is bad enough in itself. But in many countries and at different times in history, laws have been passed based upon beliefs regarding the nature of human differences. Some of these laws, based upon misunderstanding and error—even honest error—have given rise to much human misery and grief.

This book will try to provide answers to certain basic questions:

1. What are the differences between human beings—as individuals and as groups?
2. Why do these differences exist?
3. Is there any relationship between one difference and another? Are blond-headed people, for example, less (or more) intelligent than brunettes or red-heads?
4. Why, after centuries of research and explanation, is there still so much confusion and disagreement about the nature and degree of human differences?

Perhaps these questions appear simple and straightforward. They are not. To deal with them properly, and to avoid adding to the confusion, we will break a few of the questions into more manageable issues.

For example, we will separate the question *What are the differences?* into those differences which are biological in nature and those which are social. That is, we will separate those which are inborn from those which reflect a different kind of upbringing or way of life.

In order to understand why confusion and misunderstanding persist (the fourth question), we will find it necessary to look into the history of man's search for explanation. In doing so, however, we will draw a line between what we shall call *the study of race* and *racism*. The basis for our distinction will be the issue of intent or motivation: What is in the mind of the person who is studying the problem? Why is he spending his time in this way?

Determining another person's intent is of course a very difficult matter; some would even argue that it is impossible ever to know. Still, in courts of law, it is often the duty of the jury to reach a decision on this very question. If one man kills another, it is very important to find out whether or not he *meant* to do it. If the jury decides that it was an accident, then the crime is called *manslaughter*. If they conclude that the killing was intentional, it is called *murder* and the punishment is greater.

What yardstick can we use to determine intent on the part of those who deal with human variation? Let us return to the Cherokee myth with which we began. It is obviously an attempt (a poor one perhaps, but that is not the point) to explain the differences among men. But note how it ends: the Indians came out just right whereas the Africans and Europeans emerged badly made, imperfect.

Often people are not fully aware of their own motives. As in the case of the Cherokee, we may find men pondering on human differences—but also trying to prove that their own kind is better than all others. In this book, however, if we are to pierce through all the confusion that exists on the subject of race, we must try to separate these two motives. For our purposes, then, we will consider anyone (however in error he may be) a student of race if we feel certain he is motivated primarily by a desire to understand or explain the differences. We will label as racism any attempt to demonstrate that *we* are better than *they*.

1

The Classification of Living Things

All living things are curious; even the simplest one-celled creature continually probes its surroundings, avoiding danger and seeking food. In this respect man is no different from the monkey, the moose, or the musk ox. Like all other animals he studies the world around him, poking his fingers, his nose, his eyes, his ears—and his mind—into everything. Like the elephant and the amoeba, he, too, would like to know whether that new thing he has just detected is edible or enemy, good or bad.

Man differs from all other living things in that he alone (as far as we know) goes beyond simple curiosity. Human beings, in all societies, try to impose order on the universe around them. In all languages, for example, there are names for everything known to the people who speak the language—all the plants and animals, every river and every mountain. The Bible, in the book of Genesis, expresses this very human quality:

> And out of the ground the Lord God formed every beast of the field, and every fowl of the air; and brought them unto Adam to see what he would call them: and whatsoever Adam called every living creature, that was the name thereof. (II;19)

But order implies more than merely assigning names. Human beings find it necessary to decide what things belong together, because they have some quality in common, and what things must be assigned to different groups. For example, horses, oaks, mice, grass, sparrows, sharks, bats, worms, whales, barracudas, and vultures are all *living things*. But we want to know much more than that.

For example, which of that group of living things are similar to one another, and which are different? To begin with, we can easily separate plants from animals: only oaks and grass are plants, all the others are animals. Still not satisfied? Oaks and grass may both be plants, you feel, but they are certainly not the same *kind* of plants.

And, while you agree that worms and whales and horses are animals, you feel we should be able to divide up the category of animals into more meaningful subgroups. Well, let us separate out the ones that swim in the sea (barracudas, whales, sharks) from the

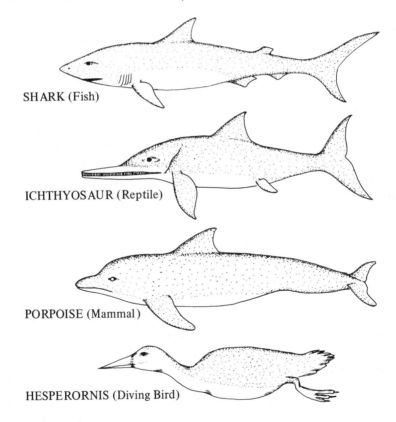

SHARK (Fish)

ICHTHYOSAUR (Reptile)

PORPOISE (Mammal)

HESPERORNIS (Diving Bird)

The shark, Ichthyosaurus, porpoise, and Hesperornia all look more or less alike, but are respectively a fish, a reptile, a mammal, and a diving bird. The shark and porpoise are modern creatures; the others are extinct.

ones that fly in the air (vultures, bats, sparrows), and from the ones that walk on the land (horses, mice). What shall we do with worms? Perhaps we must set up a special category of those that burrow under the ground. Otherwise, are the above categories satisfactory?

Not entirely. Biologists point out that while whales swim like fishes and bats fly like birds, the most significant thing about them, at least to the biologists, is that both bear their young alive and nurse them—just like horses and mice—and so the biologists prefer to classify all of these four together, as mammals, however different they may look to us. Barracudas and sharks, furthermore, may look more or less alike, but it turns out they are much less closely related than we might suspect. (Barracudas are true bony fishes; the "bones" of sharks, however, are actually cartilage hardened by lime.)

If we wish to classify things there are certain questions we are going to have to answer: How many classes do we need? What reason do we have for putting things in the same class—or insisting they belong in different classes? Scientists say, "What is your *criterion?*" or, if you have more than one, "What are your *criteria?*" Some might say that it is sufficient if two things look alike—like sparrows and bats, or whales and sharks—or if they behave in a similar way in that both fly, or both swim. Other people, however, insist that these are only superficial, or surface, similarities, and we must not allow ourselves to be misled by such unimportant similarities or differences. Basic biological features, like how creatures bear their young, the ability to regulate body temperature, the structure of the heart, and so on, are much more important, even if they are not easily detected.

Finally, another question appears to have crept into our attempt to classify those living creatures. Grass and oaks, we said, were more closely related to one another than they were to any of the others no matter how different they look. Barracudas and sharks may look alike but still they are only distantly related. What do we mean, then, by *distantly related?* When we say that you and your brother or sister are related we mean you both have the same set of parents. But what do we mean when we say that the whale, the bat, and the mouse are more closely related to each other than any of them are to the shark, the vulture or the worm? Obviously we don't mean that the bat and the whale have parents in common. But are we implying that they are descended from the same set of *ancestors?* And if we are saying that, how do we know?

And how about those living things which are dearest of all to human beings, namely human beings? Are they so different from other living things as to constitute a class apart? Or are they to be classified along with other living things? Are they animals—along with worms? Are they mammals—along with bats and mice?

Uncomfortable as such classifying may make us feel, it appears that we belong among the mammals and, with other mammals, among the animals. Does that mean we are related to whales and vultures? If so, who are our closest relatives? These are all questions to be pursued in this book.

There is yet another question that those who would classify human beings are likely to ask. Are there different kinds of humans? And if so, how many different kinds are there? All the other questions we raised earlier about classifications of living things apply to this problem as well. How many classes (types? races?) shall we set up? What criterion for classification shall we use—the way people look? Or must we seek something of greater biological significance? And, finally, who is related to whom, and how closely?

CLASSIFYING HUMAN BEINGS

We have seen that humans tend to order and classify, and so of course we may expect they will try to classify human beings. The ancient Hebrews, convinced that man was created once, in the form of Adam, and that all living humans were descended from this one common ancestor, were satisfied that all men were related. They divided humanity into three groups, each descended from one of the three sons of Noah: the Semites descended from Shem, the Hamites descended from Ham, and the Japhites from Japheth. It is of some interest to note that the ancient Hebrews, as far as we can now tell, set up their system of classification in order to decide how closely (or how distantly) they were related to the various tribes or peoples (the Canaanites, the Jebusites, the Cushites, etc.) with whom they were in contact. Although that particular question is not of very great interest to most people today (outside of specialists in the ancient Middle East), the ancient Hebrews did in fact make certain lasting contributions to the classification of living things in general, and of human beings in particular. The question of relationship—as we have seen—is still being investigated, and became particularly important once Charles Darwin (1809–1882) introduced the concept of evolution. We'll have something to say about evolution later in the book.

While scholars today rarely seek to find out who are the sons of Shem and who the sons of Ham, the words *Semitic* and *Hamitic* are still very much in use. (*Japhite,* however, appears to have gone out of use.) Whether the words *Semite* and *Hamite* can properly be used to classify human groups (or "races") is currently the subject of argument; but those who study languages agree there is a Semitic family of languages (Hebrew, Arabic, and a number of others), and some scholars also believe there is a Hamitic Family as well (Ancient Egyptian and other languages in Africa).

The notion of classifying people according to languages appears to have begun with the ancient Greeks. They divided the world into those who spoke the various dialects and languages recognizable as Greek (the Ionians, the Achaeans, the Macedonians, the Thessalonians, and so on) and those who spoke barbarian languages. The word *barbarian* was applied to anything that was not Greek. For the Greeks heard all foreign languages as a lot of strange noises, which sounded to them like "bar-bar," and which led to their use of the term.

Amusingly, the English expression, "It's all Greek to me," is synonymous with "I don't understand a word he is saying." And this is exactly what the Greeks meant when they called someone a "barbarian." The word "barbarian" has stayed with us, however, though it now means something other than a person who cannot speak Greek.

But people not only talk differently—they differ also in shape, in skin and hair color, and so on. The ancient Egyptians were very much aware of these differences, as we can tell from their paintings. But their paintings and drawings show something very interesting. All kings and nobles, for example, were represented by large figures, while slaves and prisoners of war were represented by tiny figures. In the same way, all Egyptians (whatever their actual skin color) were represented as having a reddish-brown skin, all Ethiopians (that is, the people living to the south of the Egyptians) were represented as having black skins. The people of the lands to the east of Egypt (Hebrews, Assyrians, etc.) were represented as having light skins and curly beards, while a people to the west of Egypt, the Libyans, were represented as having white skins and yellow hair.

It is true that the people who live today in the lands south of Egypt are in general somewhat darker than the people of Egypt, while the people of Egypt are in turn somewhat darker than those who live to the east or west of them. The Egyptians tend to be

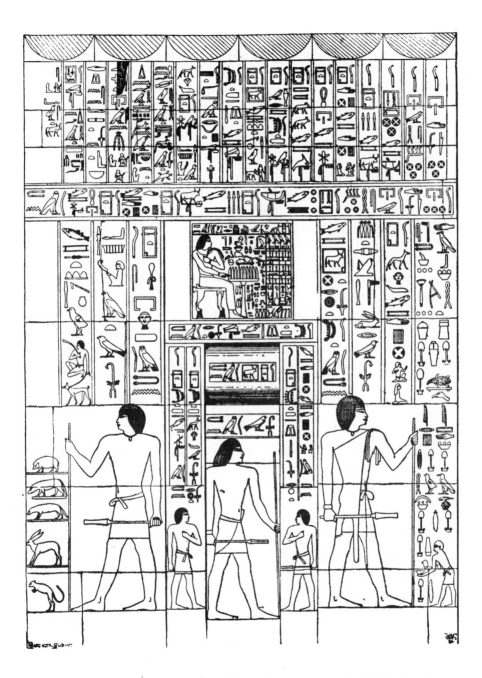

The ancient Egyptians revealed the class structure of their society by depicting "important" personages larger than others.

somewhat less hairy (or less heavily bearded) than the Arabians or others to the east, while the occasional appearance of light skin and blond hair has been noted in Morocco and other parts of North Africa. Nevertheless, it is important for us to note that these characterizations are by no means true of *all* the people living in any of the areas mentioned. There are bearded men in Egypt and men in Arabia who cannot grow beards. There are men in Egypt and Morocco as dark as or darker than some in Ethiopia. Very likely, this state of affairs was as true for the region three thousand years ago as it is today. The Egyptians, in other words, not only classified people by what they considered strikingly different aspects of their appearance, but they represented *all* the people of a given place as having the same physical characteristics. They couldn't cope with all the actual variations—so they simply ignored them. And that has been true of most attempts to classify humans from the time of the ancient Egyptians to the present.

Other peoples, in other places and times, have classified human beings in other ways, using criteria that seemed important to them. Hindus, in classical India, believed in reincarnation—that is, that the human soul was immortal and would transfer from the body of a dying person to some newborn infant and thus live life after life on earth. They believed, further, that the life a person led would determine the nature of his next reincarnation. In other words, if one was a good, kind, pious person for a whole lifetime, one's soul would be reborn into a higher body, while the soul of an evil person would be reborn into a lower body. What was *higher* and what was *lower?* Hindus believed that mankind (that is, the people of India, the only mankind they knew) was divided into four groups, ranked from highest to lowest in terms of how pure their souls were. Those in the highest category (the *Brahmans*) were so pure-souled that they were almost divine. Those in the lowest (the *Sudra*) were so impure of soul ("polluted") that higher-ranked people could not take food from them or even touch them at the risk of having some of the pollution rub off on them.

Scientific Classification

Modern classification (or scientific classification) of human beings may be said to have its origins in the work of Carl von Linné, who is remembered by the Latin form of his name, Linnaeus, for he wrote in Latin as did most scholars of his time. Linnaeus, who was born in Sweden in 1707 and died in 1778, actually did much more than

Two young schoolgirls in India. *United Nations.*

classify human beings; he was a naturalist who devised a system for classifying *all* living things, and though science has learned much since his time, the Linnaean Taxonomic System is still in use today. Naturally, with increasing information and understanding, some of his classifications have had to be modified or changed.

Linnaeus traveled widely, collecting and describing plants and animals. The problem he attempted so brilliantly to solve in his famous book, *Systema Naturae* (1737) (*The System of Nature*), is one that any person who loves the fields and woods would understand. Suppose, in your rambles, you catch a butterfly or pick a flower of a kind you have never seen before. You would like to know if anyone has ever before seen one of these, and if so, what it is called.

On the other hand, if you are the first to notice it, perhaps you would like to name it—but how can you choose a name that you can be sure others will be willing to accept? In other words, how can we work out a system of naming living things that all scholars can agree on? Further, we want to make it possible for all the names to be arranged in some logical way in books and in museum collections so that students can learn the names and be able to check with ease whether or not they have discovered something entirely new.

Linnaeus suggested that all living things be assigned two names, a *species* name and a *genus* name. Hence his system is often called a *binomial*—two-named—taxonomic system. The word *species* (spee'-shees) comes from a Latin word meaning things of the same appearance, form, or kind. The word is the same for both singular and plural: we say one species and ten species just as we say one sheep and ten sheep. *Genus* (jee'-nus) comes from a Greek word that originally meant much the same thing as species (the same kind, related things). The plural of genus is *genera* (jen'-er-a), so we speak of one genus but of two genera.

Though the words originally meant much the same thing in two different languages, since the time of Linnaeus they have come to be used for very different levels of classification of nature. A *species* has come to mean the largest group of a particular life form capable of producing offspring (children) that are viable—that is, that will be born alive and will in turn be able to have children. This definition doesn't hold too well for many one-celled creatures (such as amoebas, which reproduce by dividing in half, and so have no offspring and no parents) and for certain plants. Here the classifiers must rely on structural and functional similarities. The definition is useful, however, for all multi-celled animal life, including insects, fish, birds, and mammals—including man.

The concept of species is important in the study of life for many, many reasons. To begin with, it provides us with a basic unit for classifying life forms. It rests upon an *objective* criterion—one which can be tested by anyone and is not affected by personal tastes and attitudes. Maybe you think a barracuda and a shark look enough alike to be classed together, but a shark and a barracuda can never mate and have children. (Why not? We'll discuss this in Chapter 10.) And so we cannot call them members of the same species. On the other hand, maybe someone else thinks a spaniel and a collie are so different in appearance that they shouldn't be classed together. A collie and spaniel *can* mate, however, and produce lots of happy pups. The pups may not have pedigrees but when they become adults they will go on reproducing themselves as long as they are allowed to. Like it or not, therefore, collie and spaniel belong to the same species, as we have defined the term, but barracuda and shark do not.

We said that members of the same species must be able to produce not only offspring, but *viable* offspring, themselves capable of having young. Horses and donkeys certainly look very much alike, and if a male donkey is mated with a female horse they are likely, in fact, to produce offspring. But the offspring of such a mating is what we call a mule, and a mule is always sterile—it can never produce a baby mule. The same thing happens when a lion and tiger are mated. We know, therefore, that the lion, the tiger, the horse, and the donkey each belong to different species.

Another reason why the concept of species is important is that it indicates the presence of an absolute barrier between two populations of creatures. Mutations, or new forms, appear from time to time in all populations, plant or animal, and if changes provide some advantage they are likely to spread throughout the population, given enough time. Suppose, for example, a horse were to be born with horns, and that this were to convey such an advantage that he lived longer and had more children than any other horse. Then, if the same were true of his children and their children, over time more and more horses would have horns. Eventually, given enough time and if we suppose that horns were of truly great advantage, all horses in the world might have horns. But horses and donkeys belong to separate species, and so we know that horses could never transmit the new trait to donkeys; there is a permanent barrier between the two species and no trait can cross from one species to another.

As we shall see in a later chapter, all living creatures are changing all the time. New traits appear, spread through part or all of a species, and in time may be replaced by some new trait. A species may be made up of many populations, separated from each other and slightly different, but as long as all the populations belong to one species the possibility exists for traits to be transmitted from one population to another. If, however, populations become so different that members of one cannot mate with members of the other, then they have become, like the lion and the tiger, two separate species which must forever pursue their separate ways.

But how can we show in our method of classification that lions and tigers, though *now* separate species, once belonged to the same species? To show that, following Linnaeus, we use the term genus: a genus is made up of a group of very similar (and, we believe, closely related) species. Linnaeus proposed, and scientists have agreed, that we begin the genus name of any creature with a capital letter, and the species name with a small letter. For the most part, we even follow his practice of using only Latin genus and species names, although very few scientists today still write in Latin. Thus, the genus of all cats is *Felis* (Latin for "cat") but the lion belongs to the species *leo* (for "lion") and the tiger to the species *tigris*. According to Linnaeus, they are both members of the same genus, but they have different full names: the lion's name is *Felis leo* and the tiger's name is *Felis tigris*. That is how their names will appear on their cages at the zoo, and if you walk on down the row of cages you are likely to come to one labeled *Felis pardis*. You recognize the creature inside as a leopard, but now you know his species name is *pardis* and he belongs to the genus *Felis* along with the lion and the tiger.

Look up the word *horse* in a good dictionary and you will discover that his classification is *Equus caballus* (both from Latin words meaning horse). The donkey, or ass, is named *Equus asinus*. And so on, for all living things.

Linnaeus was aware, too, that some genera are more similar to one another than they are to others, and he proposed that, just as similar species are classed in one genus, similar genera be classed in one *order*. Linnaeus, and scholars who came after him, made other suggestions for classifying living things and for rearranging the classifications that had been made. It is unlikely that creatures placed in two species originally will later be lumped into one, or that one species will be divided into two (although, occasionally, such things can happen). It often happens, however, that as more knowledge is accumulated scientists change their minds about whether or not two species belong to the same genus. Many new terms (*kingdom, phylum, family, tribe, etc.*) have come into use for groupings larger than the genus, and the prefixes *sub-* and *super-* (*subphylum, superfamily, etc.*) are used for special problems in classification.

Another question has been of concern to all taxonomists (classifiers) from Linnaeus to the present: Is there any unit smaller than the species? Since all members of a species are capable, normally, of breeding with other members, this is often a difficult question to answer. What may seem to be important differences among members of a species to one scientist may seem unimportant to another. Are the differences (for example, between the common brown bear and his cousin, the giant grizzly) signs that the species is on the way to dividing into two new species, or are they just minor adjustments to differences in climate or food supply?

You can imagine the endless arguments scholars can have about such things. Some scientists are satisfied to say that a species is made up of *populations*—a group of individuals more likely to mate with one another than with members of other populations. If you have rats living on five islands, for example, you would speak of the rat population of each island. This is because a rat usually finds its mate on its own island, unless it happens to be washed out to sea and makes it to another island alive. Some scholars try to decide whether they can divide a species into *subspecies*—those populations which are apparently on their way to becoming new, and separate, species.

It must be remembered that Linnaeus lived in the eighteenth century, a hundred years before Charles Darwin and the concept of evolution. Since Darwin's time, we now say that species are members of the same genus because they are related—as in the case of horses and donkeys. Similarly, we think of subspecies as on their way to becoming new and separate species.

Linnaeus knew nothing of this. He believed, as far as we can tell, that all living things existed, *unchanging,* as they had been created in the beginning. He grouped species into one genus, not because he thought they had common ancestors some time in the past (at least, he never gave that as a reason), but because they seemed very similar to him. In the same way, he noticed differences within a single species, but he was apparently not interested in whether or not the subgroups of the species were—or were not—developing into new species. These were matters of interest to Darwin, and to later scholars.

For the subgroups of a species, therefore, Linnaeus used a concept which has come to be translated in English as *race*. The word *race,* according to the Oxford English Dictionary, has been in use in English since around 1500, and goes back to a Spanish word *raza* which the dictionary tells us is "of obscure origin." Thus we don't know where it came from before that, or what it meant originally. Now, it has come to mean many things: a breed, a tribe, a stock, and—most particularly—a division of a species.

Linnaeus, then, as part of his effort to classify all living things, also classified man. He named him, according to the binomial system of classification, *Homo sapiens.* You know how to read this now. He assigned man to the genus *Homo* (from the Latin word for "man," naturally) and to the species *sapiens* (from the Latin word for "wise"). We will return later to the question of who else, if anyone, is in the genus *Homo* with us, and it may be too early as yet to ask whether our species is entitled to the name *sapiens*.

For now, let us note that Linnaeus was aware that not all humans look like all other humans. Like the Egyptians before him, he divided mankind up according to skin color, and reported that there were four divisions, or races, of man:

Homo sapiens Africanus negreus (black African *Homo sapiens*)
H. sapiens Americanus rubescens (red American *H. sapiens*)
H. sapiens Asiaticus fucus (darkish Asian *H. sapiens*)
H. sapiens Europeus albescens (white European *H. sapiens*)

These divisions did not stand the test of time and underwent much revision in the years to come. It is important to note, one more time, that for Linnaeus these races are divisions of the human species, neither more nor less. For him, it was not important whether they were or were not closely related; or which of these races derived from common ancestors; or whether or not any of them were subspecies on their way to becoming new species.

Those were issues that were raised later, as we shall see.

2

Recent Classifiers of Man

Linnaeus' scheme for classifying all living things—his binomial taxonomic system—was eagerly accepted and followed by naturalists and other scientists who came after him. His terms species and genus are in common use in biology today. True, some new terms have been introduced, and some of his arrangements of species and genera have been reorganized. And when Darwin's concept of evolution came to be accepted, other changes had to be made; new definitions and new criteria for grouping creatures together came into use, for the question of relationship took on new importance. Nevertheless, if Linnaeus were to come to life today and were to read textbooks on botany and zoology he would recognize not only his old system but even most of the names of species and genera. His proposals, though more than two hundred years old now, have for the most part stood the test of time.

His suggestions for the divisions (races) of mankind, however, were not accepted. Within his own lifetime other scholars were finding the races of man, as proposed by Linnaeus, to be unsatisfactory, and were suggesting different divisions.

To begin with, Linnaeus named only four groups, representing the populations of Africa, Europe, Asia, and the New World (the Indians of North and South America). What of Australia, the South Seas, the East Indies, and other places in the world? Were the populations of these areas to be included in one or another of the four races of Linnaeus, or were they to be considered *additional* races? More troublesome was the fact that almost every one of the divisions Linnaeus had proposed included people who didn't exactly belong—*according to the very criteria suggested by Linnaeus himself!*

Linnaeus classified people, you will remember, on both the basis of skin color and of the continent on which they lived. One division, for example, was *the black-skinned people of Africa.* But the ancient Egyptians, we pointed out earlier, had noted *three* different and characteristic skin colors in Africa—and they weren't even describing the entire continent! As for the *white-skinned people of Europe,* was this meant to include the Lapps, a reindeer-herding people in northern Scandinavia? The Lapps certainly lived in Europe but in appearance they resembled the people of northern Asia more than they did the other people of Europe. And what of the people of southwest Asia (otherwise known as the Middle East or Asia Minor)? Many of them were certainly similar to Europeans in appearance, but they didn't live in Europe.

Some scholars argued that there was enough difference among the inhabitants of Europe (even apart from the difficult question of the Lapps) to warrant dividing Europeans into three or more races, and over the years the terms *Nordic* (for northern European), *Alpine* (for central European), and *Mediterranean* (for southern European) came into use. What about the Jews of Europe, some asked? Were they to be considered of the European race just because they lived in Europe, or were they to be assigned to their place of origin, Asia Minor, and whatever racial category was assigned to the people of that area?

An even more difficult problem was posed by the peoples of India and China. True, they all lived in Asia, but the category *darkish-skinned people of Asia* (Linnaeus: *H. sapiens Asiaticus fuscus*) was a difficult one to interpret. *Fuscus* can mean anything darker than white but not quite black. It can be used, for example, to refer to the time of the day we call dusk—when the bright sunlight has disappeared, but it is not yet the deep darkness of night. Do the Chinese have darkish skins, or are they not, rather, a light yellowish tan, not so very much darker than many Europeans? Many people in India, on the other hand, are quite dark—in south India there are people as dark-skinned as many of those who live in Africa.

The category *red-skinned people of America* presented other problems. Apart from the fact that this so-called race included all the

American Indians, from Alaska to Tierra del Fuego at the tip of South America (a bunching together of many different appearing populations), was it meant to include all the descendants of Europeans and Africans who had come to live in North and South America? They were all *"Americans"* now, after all!

In 1775, the year before the thirteen colonies in North America declared their independence from England, a new proposal for classifying the varieties of mankind appeared in print. In that year, Johann Friedrich Blumenbach (1752–1840), a German doctor who was particularly interested in comparative human anatomy (the study of differences and similarities in human bodies), published a book entitled *De Generis Humani Varitate Nativa* (published in English under the title: *On the Natural Variety of Mankind*). Blumenbach is often referred to as the "father of racial classification" and certainly with the publication of this book, he introduced the study of *physical anthropology*. (Anthropology means the study of man; physical anthropology is a subdivision which is concerned with the origins of man and the nature of—and reasons for—the differences in appearance and shape of different groups of men in the world today. Another subdivision is *cultural anthropology*, which is concerned with human societies.)

Blumenbach's proposals for dividing mankind into races came as a result of much study and research. He had, for example, a very large collection of human skulls, from all parts of the world, and he developed important techniques for the study and measurement of them.

According to Blumenbach, mankind was divided into five races. His names for them, translated into modern English, were: *Caucasian, Mongolian, Ethiopian, Malayan,* and *American.* His categories, as we shall see, did not solve all the problems we have mentioned, but they were certainly more useful than the ones proposed by Linnaeus, and some of the names he proposed have continued to be used to the present time.

The category *Ethiopian* included all the people of Africa living south of the Sahara desert, plus all of their descendants in other parts of the world. Their most important distinguishing feature was considered to be their skin color—described as black—although Blumenbach, and other scholars later, believed they also had certain distinguishing features of skull shape, hair shape, etc.

For this reason, and also perhaps because the word *Ethiopian* can be confusing (it could refer just to a person who lives in the country of Ethiopia, in East Africa, or to someone from some other part of

At left is a representative of Australia's original population.
Below are three girls from the Philippines. According to Blumenbach's classification they would be members of the same "Malayan" race!

Australian Information Service and *Philippine Association.*

Africa), the category Ethiopian was soon changed to *Negro* (from the Latin word for "black"). Note that the name African—used by Linnaeus—had to be dropped by Blumenbach and those who came after him because they didn't want to include in the same race the people of North Africa, who are, after all, also Africans! Moreover, they wanted to be able to include in their scheme members of this Negro race who were now living elsewhere in the world, particularly in the New World.

Blumenbach's *American* race was essentially the same as the one for which Linnaeus had used the same name: all the original inhabitants of North and South America, and their descendants. Not enough was known about them, as yet, for problems in classifying them to be seen. On the other hand, Blumenbach advised dividing into two races that enormous population that Linnaeus had seen as one race, *Asiaticus fuscus*.

For Blumenbach, there was a Malayan race, made up of the Malayan-speaking peoples of Malaya, the Philippines, and other islands and territories of what we now call southeast Asia, as well as the original inhabitants of Australia, New Guinea, and others who speak non-Malayan languages. Their common distinguishing feature, therefore, was not common language, but varieties of brown skin, ranging from light to dark.

In Asia, according to Blumenbach, there was also to be found a Mongolian race, made up of the so-called "yellow-skinned" peoples of China, Japan, and of eastern and northern Asia.

The final race proposed by Blumenbach was the *Caucasian*—made up of the peoples of Europe, the population of North Africa, and the population of southwestern Asia (Asia Minor) eastward until we find ourselves among representatives of the Mongolian or Malayan races.

PROBLEMS IN SETTING UP CATEGORIES

Some of the difficulties encountered by Linnaeus, Blumenbach and others in attempting to set up reasonably accurate racial categories have already been mentioned. These difficulties (and others, to be discussed) made it a problem even to find acceptable *names* for the racial categories. We have already seen how the term *African* became unsatisfactory because it implied all people living on the African continent, and not everyone living there seemed to belong. We have seen how African was changed to Ethiopian, which in turn was found unsatisfactory because Ethiopian also means a citizen of

Ethiopia. Then came the change to Negro. Even this last term wasn't satisfactory, because the category it is used to cover includes people, such as the Bushmen and Hottentots of South Africa, who are really more brown than black. In recent years, in fact, scholars prefer to say *Negroid,* which means Negro-like.

American was given up as a racial label because the word is used today for *any* inhabitant of North and South America. It is also used by citizens of the United States, for themselves alone, somewhat to the irritation of their neighbors in the New World! Few Americans are descendants of the original inhabitants. Indian isn't such a good word either since it also means a citizen of India. Some scholars took to the term *American Indian,* and some even contracted this name to *Amerind.* As more came to be known about the American Indians, many differences of opinion arose about their racial classification. It was pointed out, as has been noted, that there were many different types to be seen among the Amerinds; the Eskimo, for example, presents a very different appearance from the Plains Indians, and both are very different from the Indians who live in the jungles of Brazil. Are all to be considered members of the same race? On the other hand, others argued that since we are fairly certain that *all* the American Indians came out of northern Asia not more than fifteen or twenty thousand years ago—and still resemble in large measure the peoples presently living in Siberia—why should we call them a separate race at all? Why not include them among the rest of Blumenbach's Mongolian race?

Mongolian, as a racial designation, is another word that reflects the difficulty of finding one name for all the people it is supposed to include. The Mongols, descended from a famous warrior folk, live to the north of China. Once, the Mongols conquered not only China but most of the continent of Asia and even parts of Europe. Even so, they are not a very numerous people, compared with the Chinese. Thus it seems a little odd to have the name of this one group extended to so many others.

Blumenbach's other term for Asiatics, *Malayan,* has not stood the test of time. It was decided early that the native population of Australia had no more similarity to Malayans than they did to Africans or American Indians, and that it was silly to include them with the people of southeast Asia. Some scholars argued that the native Australians should be placed in one of the existing racial categories, such as Caucasian. Others considered them to be a distinct and separate race, the Australian. This name, in turn, was eventually changed to Australoid in order to include some similar-appearing groups scattered from southern India to New Guinea. The rest of the people considered Malayan by Blumenbach had to be given places in the racial classification scheme, too. Most of the peoples actually speaking Malayan languages were eventually included with the Mongolian group to the north. Since this race eventually was considered to include Chinese, Japanese, Siberian peoples (including *real* Mongols!), Southeast Asians, Polynesians, American Indians, and many more, you will not be surprised to learn that the name was changed to *Mongoloid* (Mongol-like) !

Blumenbach's final choice of racial names—Caucasian—is particularly interesting. We can see the problems he faced in finding an adequate name for this racial category. He couldn't call its members Europeans, as Linnaeus had done, since he wanted to include populations from northern Africa and eastern Asia. He couldn't call them White-skinned people either. After all, skin colors among the peoples included in this category ranged from an absence of any color (really a pinkish color, because the tiny blood vessels under the skin show through) through tan to a fairly dark brown. What tribal, or language, or national, name would possibly be even slightly representative of all these different peoples? He decided, finally, to name them *all* after the Caucasus Mountains, which are located in what is today southern Russia, and which are considered by some to form a sort of natural boundary between Europe and southwestern Asia. Did he choose *Caucasian* because the mountains represent a point between at least two of the divisions of the race? It is difficult to know for certain. Many other explanations of his choice of terms have been offered. Did Blumenbach think, as some have said, that Mount Ararat—the mountain on which, according to the Bible, the Ark of Noah and his sons Shem, Ham and Japheth was supposed to have landed—was located in the Caucasus range? It would seem unlikely that a scholar as learned as Blumenbach would make such a mistake, for Mount Ararat is actually located in what is presently the eastern part of Turkey. It has been said that Blumenbach considered one of the peoples of the Caucasus—known as the Georgians—to be among the most attractive in the world. It is also said that he was particularly fond of an exceptionally fine skull in his collection, which came from the Caucasus region. Whatever his reasons, he did choose the name Caucasian for this race—and the name has stayed with us to the present time, although in recent years slightly modified, as you might expect, to *Caucasoid*.

Although Blumenbach is entitled to be called the "father of racial classification" his was certainly not the last word on the subject. Many scholars—anatomists, physical anthropologists, and others—tried their hands at the solution of the many problems facing anyone who would attempt to classify mankind. As we have seen, additions and subtractions were proposed for Blumenbach's list of races. For many scholars, the important thing was to find better criteria for determining into which race people were to be classified. We have seen that the continent on which people live and skin color—the first two criteria proposed by Linnaeus—were not entirely satisfactory. Some continents seemed to contain representatives of more than one race and some races were to be found on more than one continent. Human skin color appears in so many bewildering shades and gradations that it too proved to be difficult to use, except in a few extreme cases.

Scientific Measurement—But of What?

Building upon the work of Blumenbach, many scientists concentrated upon measurements of the human skull. Did each race have a characteristic skull shape (or shapes)? If this were so, and could be proved, they felt, it would be necessary only to measure the shape of a person's skull to know his racial classification. Even more important, many scholars, including historians, were interested in finding out what peoples lived in different places in the world in ancient

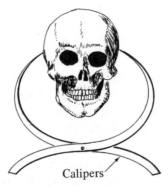

Measuring cephalic index. Calipers are used.

times. Unfortunately, the only evidence they had, in many cases, consisted of a few pieces of skeletal material from some ancient graveyard. Imagine how useful it would be if the race of the original person could be determined by measuring his skull!

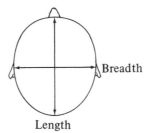

(Top of head, looking down)

Top of head, looking down. Measurements for cephalic index are taken of the greatest length and breadth of the head.

By 1849, the notion of *cephalic index* (cephalic comes from a Greek term meaning "of the head") had come into existence. Using a measuring instrument called calipers—shaped something like ice tongs—the scientist measured the point of widest breadth of the head or skull, that is, from ear-side to ear-side. He then measured the point of greatest length, from front to back. Measurement was in centimeters. A simple arithmetical formula then provided the cephalic index (C.I.) : C.I. equals head breadth divided by head length multiplied by 100.

$$\text{C.I.} = \frac{\text{head breadth}}{\text{head length}} \times 100$$

So, for example, if a skull had a breadth of 16 cm. and a length of 20 cm. the cephalic index would be 80.

$$\text{C.I.} = \frac{16}{20} = \frac{4}{5} = .8 \times 100 = 80$$

If a person has a cephalic index below 75, it means that his head is considerably longer than it is broad. The term for such a head or skull is *dolichocephalic* (from the Greek, meaning "long-headed"). If the cephalic index is 80 or more, it means the person is *brachycephalic* ("broad-headed"). A cephalic index between 75 and 80 is termed *mesocephalic* ("medium-headed"). It was discovered, by those who measured heads in the nineteenth century, that northern Europeans (*Nordics*) tended to be long-headed while southern Europeans (*Mediterraneans*) tended to be either round-headed or medium-headed. Eagerly, physical anthropologists began to measure heads and skulls all over the world. Any scientist, studying any group for any reason, was expected to measure all the heads available and come back with enough information to determine the average cephalic index of the group.

For a while, it was hoped that cephalic index would provide the looked-for criterion of racial membership—a criterion that could be measured, that remained the same throughout the person's life, and that was passed on to his descendants. Certainly, skin color had turned out to be unsatisfactory from the point of view of objectivity; for observers were continually disagreeing as to what kind of skin should be called brown and not black, or white and not brown. In addition, skin color changes continually; it is not constant. This changing occurs not only because of exposure to the sun, but because of health, age, and other reasons.

Cephalic index did pass the test of objectivity, and to some extent that of constancy. Nevertheless, it was not a very good indicator of race, people began to discover. Humans on different continents, assigned by the classifiers to different races, often turned out to have the same head shapes, while people on the *same* continent and assigned to the *same* race turned out to have different head shapes. We saw, for example, that northern and southern Europeans tend to have different head shapes. Does this mean they belong to different races? Some scholars argued that Nordic and Mediterranean were in fact different races. Then it was discovered that West Africans (assigned to the Negroid race) tended to be even more long-headed than northern Europeans. Did that mean northern Europeans and West Africans were to be assigned to the same "Dolichocephalic" race? Scholars began to look for other criteria.

Many others were considered. Some were discarded quickly, others pursued for a long time. Ernst Heinrich Haeckel, a nineteenth century German biologist, suggested that differences in hair type might be of racial significance. Some people, such as the Chinese, have for the most part very straight hair, while others such as Europeans often have wavy hair, and still others such as West Africans are usually found to have very curly hair. The appearance differs because of differences in the shape of the individual hair: a hair that is perfectly round in cross-section will tend to lie straight; one that is a narrow oval will tend to curl tightly; and one that is of an in-between shape will simply be wavy.

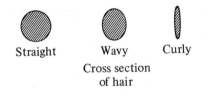

Straight   Wavy   Curly

Cross section
of hair

Cross sections of human hair.

Again, much measurement took place, and again the results were not entirely satisfactory. People with very curly hair were noted in parts of Africa and also in Melanesia (including New Guinea and other nearby islands) and the South Seas. Otherwise, the people of these different places did not look very much alike, and there was no evidence they were related. On the other hand, straight-haired people were found in eastern Asia, in the Americas, in Europe, and elsewhere. Wavy-haired people (considered a sub-division of straight-haired) were found particularly in parts of Europe and among the original inhabitants of Australia.

P. Topinard, a French physical anthropologist of the nineteenth century, proposed the measurement of *nasal index,* based on the shape of the base of the nose. Using smaller calipers than would be needed to measure the skull, Topinard measured the nose at its widest points (in millimeters). He concluded that nose widths fell into three categories, which he called the *leptorrhine* (from Greek, meaning narrow or thin nose); the *platyrrhine* (broad nose); and the *mesorrhine* (medium-sized nose). Hoping this would turn out to be the kind of criterion of racial membership that scholars were

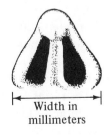

Width in
millimeters

Measuring the nasal index.

searching for, he suggested that Europeans were members of the leptorrhine race, Africans were members of the platyrrhine race, and Asiatics were members of the mesorrhine race. Again, much study and measurement over the world demonstrated that nasal index was no better than any of the other criteria for determining racial membership. Broad noses are found throughout the world among people who live in the tropics—from Africa to southern India to New Guinea to Brazil. Narrow noses are associated with cold climates; northern Europeans have a low average nasal index, but Eskimos have the narrowest noses in the world. In between, all over the world, we find medium-sized noses.

And so the search went on: ear shape, eye shape, eye color, hair color, and on and on.

Where, then, do scholars stand today on the question of how many races of man there are? Well, they don't stand together, that much is sure! Many would argue that we should give up all such efforts to determine human "races"—maybe there really are no such things. Others, however, still insist that, difficult as the whole thing seems to be, there are reasonably clear-cut divisions of mankind to be seen, and they can be marked out, along with certain problem areas. Today, many books found in public libraries and schools still refer to *three* basic races (sometimes called major stocks) of mankind: the Negroid (following Blumenbach, made up of the original peoples living in Africa south of the Sahara, plus their descendants all over the world, including the American Negroes); the Caucasoid (again, following Blumenbach, made up of the original inhabitants of Europe, North Africa and the Near East, and parts of western Asia including northern India, plus their descendants elsewhere, as in North America and Australia); and the Mongoloid (including the various peoples of eastern and southeastern Asia, plus the original inhabitants of North and South America and the South Seas).

Even among those scientists who accept these categories, there are still disagreements. The original inhabitants of Australia (usually referred to as the Australian *aborigines*) are one source of disagreement. They are dark-skinned (so some would assign them to the Negroid race), but they have wavy hair which is sometimes brown and even blond (so some would assign them to the Caucasoid race). In South Africa are found a number of very interesting groups of people who also cause assignment problems. These include the so-called *Bushmen* of the Kalahari Desert and the related *Hottentots* who were once widespread over the southern end of the continent.

Because they live in Africa south of the Sahara the tendency is to include them in the Negroid race, but some of their features are reminiscent of Mongoloids and in some ways they just look like themselves and not like anyone else. There are still other problems: the Ainu of Japan, a remnant of the people who lived there before the ancestors of the present Japanese came, who look more like Europeans (Caucasoids) than they do like Mongoloids—but who also look a little like Australian aborigines.

FIVE ORIGINAL "RACES?"

The most recent attempt to deal with these problems, and still keep as close as possible to the original classifications, was that of Carleton Coon, a distinguished American physical anthropologist. In his book *The Origin of Races* (1962), he suggests that we can best understand the present distribution of human types by looking at the

A husband and wife of the Japanese Ainu. *Japan National Tourist Organization.*

types of mankind to be found in the world during the period from about 35,000 years ago to 1500 A.D. If we go back before 35 or 40,000 years ago, Coon feels, we are no longer talking about *Homo sapiens,* but about the *ancestors* of *Homo sapiens,* so that while we may see signs of where the present races came from, we would not really be talking about the "races of *Homo sapiens*." On the other hand, he argues, after about 1500 A.D.—that is, after the explorations of Christopher Columbus, Vasco da Gama, and many others—people started moving about the face of the earth. So much intermarrying took place that since 1500 A.D. racial divisions have become blurred and confused.

Coon feels, however, that it is possible to get a clear picture of races if one focuses on the time between 35,000 years ago and 1500 A.D. In other words, even though there were great movements of people and changes in population, basic racial divisions remained clear and essentially unchanged during this whole period.

Carleton Coon proposes, therefore, that when *Homo sapiens* first appeared on the scene some 35,000 years ago *as Homo sapiens,* he was already divided into *five* races, each of which had made the transition to *Homo sapiens* at a different time and place. Each therefore was distinct from all others. Very possibly, each race was made up of about the same number of people as each of the others. In any case, the total human population could not have been very large.

Coon suggests that one race, the Caucasoid, was to be found at that time around the shores of the Mediterranean Sea (that is, in northern Africa, southern Europe, and western Asia) with perhaps a few groups as far north in Europe as the receding galciers permitted, and a few others in central Asia as far as present-day Iran (Persia). In eastern Asia, Siberia (northern Asia), and the mainland of southeastern Asia there was a second group, the Mongoloid race. In India, however, and in some of the islands of present-day Indonesia, and stretching perhaps as far as New Guinea and Australia, there was a third group, which he labels the Australoid race. In Africa, in the southern part of the Sahara Desert and the grasslands north of the tropical jungle there was a fourth group, which he suggests we call the Congoid race (from the Congo River, which was to the south of them, and which they were to reach later). Finally, he feels, there was a fifth group in Africa, about which not too much is known. Perhaps they lived in the Sahara Desert (before it dried up completely), or perhaps they lived elsewhere, alongside the Congoid peoples and between them and the Caucasoids to the north. These last he calls Capoid (partly after the Cape of Good Hope in South Africa, for he believes the Capoids were the forerunners of the Bushmen and Hottentots).

Over the thousands of years many changes occurred, Coon feels. The Capoid race wandered south in Africa and were gradually crowded into a corner by the expanding Congoid race. Similarly, the Caucasoid peoples to the north, with the coming of domestication, spread throughout Europe and the Middle East and eventually into India, pushing the Australoid people southward. In eastern Asia, Mongoloid people were also spreading. First, ancestors of the American Indians left Siberia and crossed the Bering Straits. More recently, southern Mongoloid peoples moved into the islands south of the Asian mainland, displacing Australoids and pushing them further south into New Guinea and Australia. Eventually, some Mongoloid people spread into the islands of Micronesia and Polynesia, until then for the most part uninhabited.

So, for Carleton Coon, the five original races of *Homo sapiens* were still with us in 1500 A.D., but had had different fortunes from the time when all were about equal in number. The Caucasoids and Mongoloids had increased enormously in number and had spread widely. The Congoids had prospered, although perhaps not as much as the first two, and had increased in numbers and spread throughout most of Africa. The Australoids and Capoids, however, had dwindled in numbers, or at least had not increased, and had been pushed into remote corners of the earth. After 1500 A.D., of course, everything became much more complicated. Europeans and Africans came to the New World in ever-increasing numbers and displaced or intermarried with the original American Indians, as well as with each other. According to Coon, other movements of peoples occurred on other continents, and so the distribution of the original five races is much changed, and there are also many new, or "mixed" races in the world.

Carleton Coon's proposals certainly provide solutions to many of the questions that had been raised. Even the Ainu could be explained, as an early and separated group of Australoids. His work, moreover, was based upon careful and thoroughgoing examination of fossil and other evidence. Nevertheless, there was great disagreement about his proposals among other scientists, and in the end they were rejected by the greater part of American anthropologists. Most physical anthropologists today prefer to approach human differences in terms of genetic variation, a topic to be discussed in later chapters.

At the end of this chapter, therefore, we are back where we were at the beginning—or at the time of Linnaeus, more than two hundred years ago! After all that work, and all those brilliant suggestions, all we seem to be able to say is this: while not all human beings look like all the other human beings, and while we can clearly see a lot of the ways in which people look different, scientists still do not agree on exactly how many kinds of mankind there are. They have not even decided what criteria we can use to assign people to one race or another. Some workers would simply like to give up and say that the problem is too hard—that there is no solution!

Why should it be so difficult? If taxonomists, following Linnaeus, were able to classify every variety of plant and animal with relatively little trouble, why should they have so much trouble doing the same thing with varieties of man?

3

The Wrong Track

In the preceding chapter, we saw how much scholarly effort has been expended in the search for clear and non-arguable criteria of "racial" membership, and for a classification of the varieties of mankind that would be acceptable to all. And we saw, finally, that after two hundred years of such effort there are still lots of problems and very little agreement. After such effort for such a long time, it is reasonable to suggest, as many scholars have in recent years, that we must be doing something wrong. Let us now try to see what that could be.

The easiest way to differentiate two types of creatures, of course, is to point to the clear presence, or absence, of a particular feature: horns, a tail, the leopard's spots, or the spaniel's floppy ears. It is much more difficult, as in the case of human types, when the differences are slight ones of degree or shade. For in this case all the samples can be arranged along an unbroken line stretching from one extreme to the other. Such a line is called a *continuum*. A good example, shown here, would be differences in human height.

Shortest   Tallest

The varieties of human head-shape, ranging from extremely dolichocephalic (very long-headed) to extremely brachycephalic (very round-headed) represent another continuum. It is true that trustworthy measurement of head shapes is easily achieved; in other words, someone else, if he does his work with accuracy, will come out with the same result. The problem is that, as with variation in human height, the cephalic indices of all human heads fall somewhere on a continuum, and the continuum has no breaks!

Faced with *any* continuum, all that a classifier can do is label the two extremes, in this case, long-headed and round-headed, and then decide the points along the continuum that seem—*to him*—worthy of note and of a separate label. As shown, one researcher, might decide to label and set off as a separate type the center point (mesocephalic or medium-headed) .

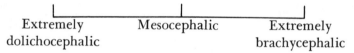

Extremely	Mesocephalic	Extremely
dolichocephalic		brachycephalic

But suppose another researcher didn't agree that the center-point was important, and (as shown) preferred to give labels to "points" one-third of the way from each end?

It is as reasonable as labeling one point in the center, or *five,* or whatever! In other words, when faced with a continuum, it is possible to make a logical argument for any number of types—from *one* to the *total number* of samples found. True, as we have seen in the cases of the continua of head shapes, nose shapes, hair shapes, and so on, most scholars tend to agree on three types (the two extremes and the midpoint) ; but not everyone agrees, and so long as there is disagreement—and no objectively correct answer—every solution is just as good as any other.

Problems of Measurement

For some criteria, the problem is compounded by the fact that *accurate* measurement is extremely difficult, if not impossible. Anything having to do with *color*—skin color, eye color, hair color—represents such a problem. People see colors slightly differently, colors look different in different lighting conditions, and it is almost impossible to reproduce accurate illustrations of fine shades of difference in colors for the researchers to take with them into the field. As a result, it frequently happens that researchers who study the same populations disagree strongly about their results. After a hundred years or more of intensive research, there is still no agreement as to exactly how many types of human skin color there are, and which human groups are characterized by which types of color. Are Australian aborigines black or dark brown? Are South African Bushmen brown or yellowish-brown? Are American Indians really red-skinned? Are Europeans really white? There is no agreement on these and many similar questions.

Furthermore, skin color—the most common criterion of racial classification—has another complicating and frustrating characteristic; the appearance or color of any person's skin is subject to a great deal of change. Certain illnesses, or the presence or absence of certain things in the diet, can cause the skin of any human to be much paler, grayer, yellower, or ruddier than would be normal for that individual. At which time of his life, or in what condition of health, are you going to measure his skin color and decide you have captured the normal tones?

As shown in the photo, the same holds for hair color.

A boy's curls at the age of five years compared with the same boy's curls at the age of eighteen. It is not uncommon for hair to change color as one grows older. *American Museum of Natural History.*

And then there is the problem of sunlight, and the human capacity to tan under exposure to the sun's rays. As far as it has been possible to tell, there is very little difference in human skin, except for the presence or absence, in the very upper layers, of a substance called *melanin* (mel'–uh–nin). Melanin consists of microscopic granules (tiny grains, or bits) of brown color. In most, though not all, human beings, there are certain cells under the surface of the skin which produce such granules of melanin. The exact service performed for the body by melanin is still not completely understood, but it is generally agreed that in some way melanin protects the skin against some of the bad effects of too much ultraviolet radiation from the sun. Among most humans, continued exposure to the sun or to other sources of ultraviolet radiation appears to stimulate the production of melanin granules, so that there are more and more of them present in the skin's upper layer. We call this process *tanning*.

The ability to tan and the amount of tanning that can take place varies from population to population and from individual to individual. In northern Europe, and particularly in Scandinavia, there are many individuals whose skins can produce little melanin—sometimes, almost none. Exposed to sunlight, their skin reddens and can acquire a painful sunburn; but no matter how long they are exposed to sunlight they never tan. In parts of Africa, and most particularly western Africa, there are people whose skin contains so much melanin that they, too, never tan. But in this case the amount of melanin has reached a maximum; it can't get any greater. Occasionally, among *all* peoples of the world, a child is born with no capacity to produce melanin. Such a child, whose skin is a pinkish-white, is called an *albino* (al–by'–no). Otherwise, all humans, including large numbers in northern Europe and throughout Africa, can tan to a greater or lesser degree.

As you can imagine, this complicates the problem of determining skin color. People of northern Europe or people whose ancestors came from northern Europe, who spend much time in the sun can often become tanned to a very dark brown. People in northern Africa or southwestern Asia, who are naturally somewhat darker than Europeans, but who wear robes and veils and try to stay out of the hot sun, may have much paler skin colors in the end than a European man who has spent some time on the beach.

Even cephalic index is subject to change, it was discovered. Early in this century, a series of studies begun by the American anthropologist Franz Boas (1858–1942) demonstrated that the average cephalic index of children of immigrants often differs from that of their parents—and even more from that of their first cousins in the old country. In other words, changes in diet and other environmental factors can affect not only skin and hair color but even the skeletal development of a person.

Measurement of "racial" differences, it can be seen, presents many problems, and in fact not all of them have been mentioned here. But there are other problems plaguing the men who would classify race, and we must turn to some of them now.

"PURE RACES"

It was pointed out earlier that since about 1500 A.D. large numbers of humans have been moving about the world, meeting other people, and that in many places there are to be found what are called "mixed races." If one uses the expression "mixed race" it certainly seems to imply that, somewhere else, there is a "pure race." For many writers on the subject of race, although for different reasons, the question of the presence or absence of a "pure race"* has been very important. The question is, what do we mean by *pure* as opposed to *mixed* when we talk about human beings?

South America is often considered a very good example of a continent having a mixed race (or even mixed races). Originally (before 1500 A.D., that is), the continent of South America was inhabited only by American Indians. Then large numbers of Europeans, mostly from Spain and (in Brazil) from Portugal, began to settle there. Soon afterward, large numbers of Africans, mostly from western Africa, were brought to serve particularly on the plantations of the Caribbean Islands and the east coast of South America. In most of the countries of South America, people living today can claim both European and American Indian ancestors. In many places, people can claim to have ancestors from Europe, Africa, as well as

* Because the authors believe that the terms "pure race" and "mixed race" are imprecise and not scientifically valid, the terms have been placed in quotation marks. It was felt, however, that continuing to do this would interfere with the flow of the text and perhaps even annoy the reader; quotation marks have therefore been omitted in what follows, but the reader is requested to keep in mind that they are implied wherever the terms appear. This holds true as well for words like "black," "white," "yellow," "Mongoloid," "Negroid," and "Caucasoid."

from the original American Indian inhabitants. Surely, they are mixed.

But—how pure is anyone else? Let us take Europe as our example. Sometime around two or three thousand years B.C. (about four or five thousand years ago) Europe was apparently invaded by a number of tribal groups speaking related languages (the ancestors of Greek, Latin, Russian, German, English and other languages spoken in Europe). We are not entirely sure where they came from, though many believe they may have come from around or near the Black and Caspian seas, in the border region between Europe and Asia. There were peoples living in Europe already, and the newcomers killed some of the earlier inhabitants and intermarried with the rest. During the period from about three to five hundred A.D. (about fifteen hundred years ago), a number of warlike peoples from central and northern Asia—the Huns, the Alans, and others—pressed into Europe, conquering and killing, and in some cases settling and intermarrying. As the Roman Empire collapsed, there was much movement of peoples. Groups from Scandinavia, such as the Goths and Vandals, moved in large numbers into southern Europe and even into northern Africa. Spain, particularly, was colonized by these northerners; *Andalusia,* the most populous region in Spain today, and located in the southern part of the country, meant originally land of the Vandals.

A few hundred years after the Vandals and Goths conquered Spain from the north, Spain was again conquered, this time by peoples coming from North Africa. By 732 A.D. the armies of the Muslim invaders controlled almost all of Spain and Portugal and had reached southern France. The Muslim religion had its beginnings in the Arabian peninsula, and the Arabs—as the first to carry the religion out into the world—were much admired. There *were* Arabs among the conquerors, of course; but a very large part of the army that conquered Spain was recruited in northern Africa, particularly in the region we now call Algeria and Morocco. Troops from what is today Mauretania (from which we get the word *Moor*) and Senegal in northwestern Africa, played an important part in the history of Spain under Islam. Eventually, Spain was reconquered by Christians and those professing to be Muslims were killed or chased out. Still, the various Muslim invaders left many descendants behind in Spain and Portugal.

Europe knew other invasions. In 1456, Turkic peoples (of Asiatic origin) conquered Constantinople and moved into the Balkan

Arabs such as this Iraqi villager and Africans such as these modern-day Senegalese played an important part in the history of Spain and Portugal. *United Nations* and *Air Afrique*.

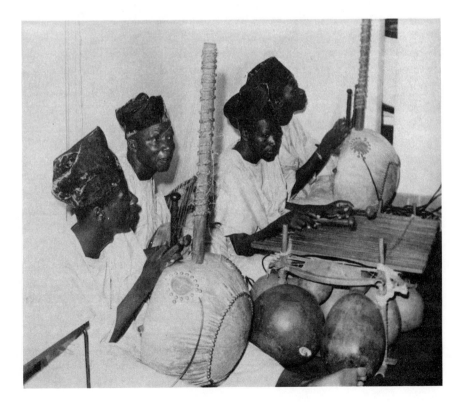

peninsula, reaching as far as Vienna, the capital of Austria, before they were stopped. Earlier, the Mongol and Tatar* armies of Genghis Khan had swept over Russia, Poland and into central Europe.

In all honesty, then, how pure were the Europeans—*before* 1500 A.D.? Is it reasonable to say that the population of South America is a mixed race while the population of Europe is a pure race?

We used Europe as our example because the history of Europe is better documented than that of other continents; but there has been just as much movement and intermarriage in Africa, Asia and in other parts of the world. The Polynesians were once considered to be a pure race (until their contact with Captain Cook and other Europeans in the eighteenth century) because they were isolated on their tiny islands. We are beginning to discover, however, through archeology and the study of languages, how the ancestors of the Polynesians moved from island to island in southeastern Asia and Melanesia, some two thousand or more years ago. Eventually they came to the uninhabited islands and atolls of the Pacific, but before that there is evidence that they intermarried with the people of almost every inhabited island they visited.

The question for those who would speak of pure as against mixed human populations is when does a mixed race become a pure race? Only if the mixture took place before 1500 A.D.? Clearly that would be silly. Try to find a good reason to support the claim that South Americans are more mixed than Europeans or Polynesians!

ORIGINAL DIVISIONS OF MANKIND?

Perhaps pure races reflect not just some earlier mixture *but the original divisions of mankind.* In other words, maybe modern Europeans do reflect centuries of invasion and mixture; but it may also be that once, if we go back far enough, their ancestors were members of one pure race or another, and so were the ancestors of all people alive on the Earth today. If most of us are mixed today, could we not have been pure once?

This concept appears to underlie most of the work on race from the time of Friedrich Blumenbach to that of Carleton Coon. It raises many questions, and cannot be answered with a simple "yes" or "no." The composition of mankind in the early days of *Homo sapiens* will therefore be discussed more fully, but in a later chapter. For now, let us consider one aspect of the problem. If we assume that

* Also called Tartar.

pure races once existed, and that traces of them can be distinguished even now, how can we determine what were the features of the pure races when they were pure? It is this question, whether or not it is phrased in this way, that is at the basis of every search for a significant criterion—for a feature we can be certain is characteristic (or was, originally) of one race only. That is, if we find it among members of a different race it proves that they had ancestors from the first one.

For example, consider black skin. Suppose, at the beginning, the human species was divided up into a number of races—three, five, or whatever—and only one of the original races was characterized by black skin. Suppose, further, that black skin could never occur in an individual who was not descended from that "race." In that case, one need only find black skin among groups or among individuals to be certain of racial ancestry. Thus, when European explorers found dark-skinned people in southeast Asia, in Melanesia (the word implies dark skin), and elsewhere, the tendency was to call such people *Negritos* or *Negrillos* and to assume that they were relatives of black Africans who had somehow become separated from the main group. It turns out, however, that dark skin is associated with extended exposure to excessive sunlight, and is characteristic of peoples everywhere in sunlit tropical regions. The question of why and how they became black will be considered later; the point is that *any* population of humans, exposed to certain conditions of sunlight for a long enough time will evolve (or change) over time in the direction of darker and darker skins—and eventually black ones. If two populations, widely separated in the world, have the same skin color, therefore, it is no proof that they are related. Perhaps they are related, perhaps they are not. All we can tell for sure is that both groups are descended from ancestors who *adapted* to conditions favoring the development of dark skins, just as the polar bear's white coat is an adaption to life amid snow and ice.

NON-ADAPTIVE TRAITS

But suppose there are features that are *non-adaptive,* that have nothing to do with climate or other external conditions, but simply represent differences? If we could find a good non-adaptive trait—wouldn't that serve to indicate racial ancestry?

The question of non-adaptive traits has always been of great interest to those studying race, but it was of particular importance to those who believed in the idea of pure races. We have seen that adaptive traits, such as skin color, are not a good indication of pure races because they seem very clearly to be responses to the environment; the fact that two widely separated populations have dark skin is by no means a clear indication that they derive from common ancestors.

But suppose two groups could be found which had the same non-adaptive trait or traits. Wouldn't this support the idea that once there were pure races, but that they have since moved, split up, intermarried, and so on? That is, those sharing the same trait or traits could then be considered descendants of the once pure race. This thought lay behind the attention given to hair form and color, eye color, and many other features, including blood types. Each of these, scholars at different times were convinced, was a true non-adaptive trait—and thus a marker of what was once a pure race.

We have already seen the difficulties in measuring any feature differentiated according to color. In addition, the populations of most parts of the world are characterized by very dark hair and eyes. In Europe, and particularly northwestern Europe (Scandinavia, the British Isles), are found most of the people with light-colored eyes and hair, so this trait is not of much use for distinguishing, say, Africans from Asiatics; for the most part they all have dark hair and dark eyes, as do a large part of the European population, including many even in Scandinavia and the British Isles! If, as in North America today, we find many people with light-colored hair and eyes, we know it is because they are descended from European colonists. But in Australia, among the original inhabitants, blondism, or at least light brown hair, has been reported among children. (As is the case with Europeans, the hair of Australian aborigines tends to darken as they grow older.) In spite of the occurrence of blondism, no convincing evidence has ever been presented that Australian aborigines are any more closely related to northern Europeans than they are to any other population in the world.

Hair shape can be measured, and it is fair to say that a large part (though not all) of the segment of mankind commonly called Mongoloid has straight hair, while most of the people commonly called Negroid have very curly hair. So far so good, but it doesn't work out quite so neatly for those called Caucasoid since both curly and straight hair is well-represented among Caucasoids—although the larger part is usually characterized as having wavy hair. Wavy, however, is something between the extremes of straight and curly; and, as we saw in our discussion of the nature of a continuum, something between two extremes tends to cover a lot of ground and include a number of differences.

The most serious question, however, is whether or not hair shape and color, and eye color, are in fact non-adaptive traits. This question has been debated for many years, with no really clear decision ever having been made. If differences in eye or hair color, or in hair shape, help—or once helped—human groups to better adapt to their physical environments, we cannot yet quite understand how. There are some hints, however: eye and hair color comes mainly from the presence or absence of melanin, and the role of melanin in protecting the skin from solar radiation is pretty clear. More and more scientists lean to the position that these traits are adaptive—that they developed among human populations as a way of helping them to adjust to their environment, for example, strong sunlight, wet or dry climate, and so on.

When differences in types of human blood were noted, some people thought that a non-adaptive, clearly detectable, racial trait had at last been found. In the nineteenth century, the technique of blood transfusion had been worked out, but doctors were reluctant to use it because the results were unpredictable. Sometimes, when the blood of one person was introduced into the circulatory system of another, the new blood mixed well and easily with the old, and the recipient was strengthened and helped in his battle for life. Other times, the new blood would refuse to mix, but would clump and remain separate, and this could lead to the death of the recipient. In 1909, Karl Landsteiner (1868–1943), an Austrian medical researcher, discovered the reason. He demonstrated that although the red cells in human blood looked identical, there were actually four types among humans. They differed according to the presence or absence of certain molecules called *antigens*. Landsteiner, in the work that was to win him a Nobel Prize, detected two different blood antigens, which he labeled A and B. People with A antigens were said to have type A blood. People with B antigens were said to have type B blood. People with neither antigen were said to have type O blood, and people with *both* antigens were said to have type AB blood. Certain types will mix, but others will not, he found.

Since Landsteiner's early work, it has been discovered that blood is even more complicated, and there are still more types, and subdivisions of types. In the first half of this century, however, these four differences in blood types were eagerly pursued by some scholars interested in studying racial differences. No one could see any possible adaptive value for the blood types; they were just "different." Furthermore, with the proper equipment a few drops of blood from a person could be analyzed, and one would know *with absolute certainty* whether that person had type A, B, O, or AB blood. Imagine how significant it would have been if *all* Africans, say, or *all* Europeans, had been discovered to have one distinct blood type—which would not mix with that of other races! In addition to providing the long-sought-for diagnostic trait of racial membership, such a trait would help to determine the racial classification of members of mixed races—simply assign a person to the race indicated by his blood type!

Alas, it was not to be. No human population, however isolated and presumably pure it may be, is characterized by only one blood type. All four types are distributed among the entire human species. Take a sample of blood types among blond, blue-eyed Norwegians, and you will soon find someone with type B blood. You can easily find another type B in a West African sample, or in a Japanese sample. Furthermore, the three persons with type B we have just found can give blood to each other—but not one of them may take blood from a close relative who has, say, type A blood! What good is this, then, for racial classification?

Early in the study of human blood types, it was noted that the types occur in different human groups in different frequencies. In other words, the number of people with one of the types may be high in one group, but very low in another. It was also discovered that type B is almost nonexistent among American Indians. Could this mean, perhaps that the original "pure" races were once each characterized by one blood type, and the mixture that we now find everywhere is simply a result of later mixing of races? The absence of type B seemed to indicate this to some, for it pointed to the possibility that the ancestors of the American Indians had migrated from Asia before the B antigens had evolved, or at least before it had spread to eastern or northern Asia.

It was then discovered that the great apes—the gorillas and the chimpanzees—share the same basic blood types with man. Although there are differences in blood chemistry which would make a transfusion between an ape and a man highly dangerous, among gorillas and chimpanzees there are essentially the same four blood types as those found among humans. But these creatures are our closest relatives among all living things—which means we are all descended from common ancestors. Therefore A, B, O and AB blood type differences, and mixed frequencies of the four types, all go back to long before the earliest human-like creatures separated from other apes!

Nevertheless, the distribution of blood types, not only the four mentioned here, but many others, is of great interest to scientists and has been carefully studied and mapped. There are many questions to be answered: Why, for example, *are* there differences? Few scientists today believe any longer in the idea of the non-adaptive trait. If blood type differences are found among humans in different frequencies in different areas, it seems to indicate that one kind of blood type has some advantage under one set of conditions, while another has some advantage under different conditions. We are not at all certain what those conditions and advantages may be. It is clear, however, that different populations in the world have markedly different frequencies of blood types. These can be charted on world maps, but the differences do not seem to be related to anything else: skin color, hair types, national boundaries, migrations of peoples, climate, or whatever.

In the case of a very few factors, such as susceptibility to certain illnesses, there are some indications of a relationship between the factor and bloodtype frequency, but there are many exceptions and problems. Otherwise, there are hardly any meaningful connections. Type A blood had a high frequency among the original inhabitants of southern Australia and the Indians of the Canadian Rockies. It is also moderately high among Europeans and Eskimos. Type B occurs in a high frequency in northern India, central and northern Asia, and is fairly high throughout Asia and in western Africa. Type O occurs in very high frequency in aboriginal South America, but there are pockets of high frequency of type O throughout the entire world. To know an individual's blood type is of no predictive value whatever in trying to determine his "racial" identification.

INDEPENDENT DISTRIBUTION OF TRAITS

The fact that blood types do not seem to associate with any other traits used for racial classification is hardly surprising. The fact is, *none* of the traits seem to associate with any of the others. Each trait—blood type, skin color, hair shape, *etc.*—has an *independent distribution*.

This simply means that physical traits distributed throughout the human species are largely independent of one another; they do not

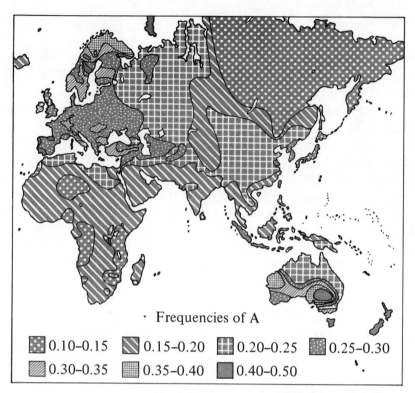

· Frequencies of A

▦ 0.10–0.15 ◩ 0.15–0.20 ▥ 0.20–0.25 ▨ 0.25–0.30
◩ 0.30–0.35 ▦ 0.35–0.40 ■ 0.40–0.50

Adapted from Mourant, *et al.*, *ABO Blood Groups*, C. C. Thomas

Frequency of blood type A versus distribution of skin color and hair form in Europe, Asia, and Africa—all before 1500. Note that Australia's original population correlates most closely with that of Europe as far as hair form is concerned, with Africa in terms of skin color, and with eastern and southern Asia in the frequency of type A blood. Japan and Korea correlate best with the rest of Asia in terms of skin color and hair form, and with Europe in distribution of type A blood.

cluster to form a racial type. In other words, if you try to set up categories of mankind on the basis of *one* trait, say, skin color, certain broad divisions do seem to emerge. If, however, you overlap the divisions indicated by *another* trait, say, hair shape, the picture gets worse, not better, and more and more confusion sets in with every additional mapping of a trait.

This alone should give us pause. Scientists have long known that when they are on the right track every additional bit of information or new discovery helps to clarify the problem, to sharpen the picture. In the search for racial criteria, the exact opposite seems to happen

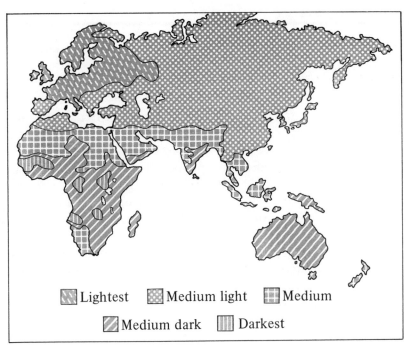

Lightest ☐ Medium light ☐ Medium

Medium dark ☐ Darkest

Adapted from Brace and Montagu, *Man's Evolution*, Macmillan

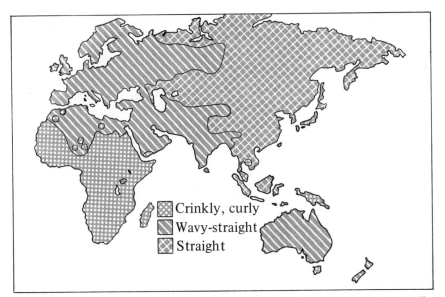

Crinkly, curly
Wavy-straight
Straight

Adapted from Brace and Montagu, *Man's Evolution*, Macmillan

every time, and that should lead us to suspect that we are not on the right track at all.

Where, then, lies the right track? We can find it if we pay close attention to what we have learned since the days of Linnaeus and Blumenbach about the nature of living things, and most particularly about *genetics*. Genetics is the study of what it is that causes the child to resemble, or in some cases *not* to resemble, the parent. Further, if we want to know how human groups are related to one another, if in fact they are, we must go back in time and study what is known of man's origins—how and why his ancestors separated from the ancestors of other creatures—and when and how man's ancestors became truly human.

In chapters to come, we will discuss these matters. First, however, we must give our attention to the topic we have labeled *racism*. The understanding of human difference is not easy. It becomes, however, even more complicated if one starts with the belief that races *must* exist, and that there *must* be pure races among them. For if, as some believe, some races are *better* than others, and if Race A (usually) one's own race) is "superior" to Race B, then to mix them would be a terrible thing. You would be taking something that was "better" and mixing it with something "worse," and the result, so it is believed by those who feel this way, cannot but be a mistake.

From the beginning, then, racists have been extremely interested in the findings of those who study race. As a result, the two subjects, racism and race, have become so intertwined that it is difficult to study one without some understanding of the other.

Let us turn, therefore, to a consideration of what is meant by racism, how it came about, and how it became so involved with the study of race.

4

On Us and Them

Bill and Joe are ten years old. They live next door to each other and have known each other since they both began to walk. They are in the same class. Today, in the school playground, the teacher has divided the boys in the class into two teams, the Blues and the Greens, and set them competing against each other in a series of sports events. Bill is a Blue and Joe is a Green. In the relay race, Joe is the last to run for his team. The Greens are behind, but Joe puts on a tremendous burst of speed and it looks as if he might just make it. Bill is leaping up and down with excitement, screaming encouragement to the Blue runner, begging him to come in ahead of Bill's old buddy, Joe: "Beat him! *Beat* him!" Bill screams.

Why?

Why should Bill want a comparative stranger to outrun his best and oldest friend? He never much liked that kid, anyway. Bill would say that for now, anyway, he is a member of the *Blue* team, and his temporary allegiance to it must outweigh his normal loyalty to his friend. Fair enough.

But what made Bill feel such allegiance? After all, an hour before he had never heard of the Blue team. The team members were chosen at random; he and Joe might easily have been on the same team, or on opposing ones. Yet, once the teams were chosen, a new loyalty came into existence, superseding all others, and Bill desperately wanted his team to win because it is *his*—and nobody wants *them* to beat *us*.

Let us stop picking on Bill. His behavior is very human. In all human societies, people distinguish between *we* and *they*. *My* clan as against yours; *my* family, *my* town, *my* nation—*my* gang against your gang. Not only does it add a certain excitement to living, as Bill and Joe are finding out, but it seems to be built into the very nature of a human group.

ETHNOCENTRISM

Ultimately, in every human society, this identification with one's own group, against all others, takes the form of *ethnocentrism*. This is a technical term deriving from two Greek words: *ethnos,* meaning "nation," and *kentron,* from which we get such words as center and central. Ethnocentrism, therefore, is the term for the feeling or belief that your own people are at the center of the universe and the only one who really count; that the way you and your people live is the only right way, and any other way of living or speaking or thinking or acting is wrong to the extent that it differs from your own.

It is *ethnocentric,* and normal enough, to believe that the accent you and your friends have, the clothes you wear and the kind of food you eat, represents the only sensible or proper way, and to be amused or disgusted at a foreigner's pronunciation, dress, or favorite dish. "Why, some of those people eat snails, or raw fish, or—would you believe it—*insects?*") Europeans have been sickened at the Chinese fondness for aged and foul-smelling eggs, and Chinese have been equally sickened at the European fondness for aged and foul-smelling milk, or *cheese,* as the Europeans call it. Everyone is comfortably satisfied that what his people do is superior.

Ethnocentrism is also reflected in the names people have for themselves, and for others. Generally, the native word in any language for the people using that language translates as "the people" or "the human being." For others, they usually have names which translate as "the strangers" or "speakers of a strange language." *Barbarian,* as we have seen, comes from a Greek word indicating that anyone who didn't speak Greek made noises that sounded like "bar-bar." *Hottentot* has a similar derivation, but from Dutch. Sometimes the name says or implies "people with disgusting habits." The word *Eskimo,* for example, was picked up by early explorers from the Algonkian Indians. In Algonkian it means "eaters of raw flesh." The people we and the Algonkians call *Eskimos* have a word in their own language for themselves: *Inuit.* It means, simply, "men." The Samoyeds, a people of northern Siberia, prefer to be called *Nentsi,* a word from their own language meaning "people." They consider *Samoyed* insulting, since in a neighboring language it means "cannibal."

And if any of you who are white-skinned happen to harbor any feelings of superiority because of that fact, you might consider this: *Oinbo* is the term for white man in Yoruba, an important language of western Nigeria. Its literal meaning is "he who has been peeled."

Ethnocentrism—a Handicap in Research

Although ethnocentrism may be a universal human condition, it can also be a serious impediment to any study of the differences between human groups. If we notice that those people on the other side of the hill look different from us—or speak or act differently—we might want to ask why there are differences, and where the differences come from. Such questions are the beginning of scientific investigation of human variation.

Unfortunately, we are all too likely (being human, and ethnocentric) to equate the difference with some kind of inferiority. Why do Africans have black skin? Why, "clearly" it is because they are closer to the apes; they evolved more recently than the Europeans and so still tend to look more like their apelike ancestors. This has actually been claimed! In the same way an African racist might use the same reasoning to explain why Europeans have more body hair than the African.

The point is that both racists are prevented by their ethnocentric assumptions from coming to grips with the basic question: Why do variations occur? How can they scientifically investigate the problem when they already believe they know the answer?

One of the first rules of scientific investigation is to question your assumptions—the things you have always believed without question until this moment. The world is flat, and if you sail to the edge you will fall off—*right?* "Well," says the scientist, "let's try it and find out."

Most people in the world, of course, are not familiar with the rules of scientific investigation, and are content to accept the assumptions of the world they know without question—and most particularly the assumption shared by almost all societies, that *we* are better than *they* are.

We have seen that the Greeks divided humanity into Greeks and barbarians on the basis of language. There is more to the story than this, however; they believed there were inborn differences in personality or character between Greeks and barbarians. They believed, in fact, that there were two types of barbarians; those who lived to the south of the Greeks in Asia Minor and Egypt, and those who lived to the north in the rest of Europe. According to the Greeks, the southern barbarians were capable of building, and living in, great civilizations (the Greeks had to believe that; all they had to do was visit the great cities of Asia Minor and North Africa!), but that the southerners had, nevertheless, a kind of slavish personality; they were incapable of living as free men and controlling their own lives. Instead they humbly allowed themselves to be ruled by cruel, despotic kings. The northern barbarians, on the other hand, were hard fighting, free warriors, as the Greeks could see. The Greeks believed, however, that the northerners were too savage ever to be able to live a civilized life.

Only the Greeks (according to the Greeks, of course) combined the best qualities of both: free, independent warriors who would

The Hereford map.

An ethnocentric world map of about 1280 A.D. In accordance with the religious beliefs of the time, Jerusalem (circle) is placed at the center of the world. *The Expansion of Europe, W. C. Abott, Holt, 1918.*

never crawl on the ground before a wicked despot, yet who were also sufficiently intelligent and industrious to build a great civilization. This happy view of the world is an ideal example of what we mean by ethnocentrism; it put the Greeks on top. They were, in their own opinion, the best in the world.

There is nothing unusual about this type of thinking; the Chinese, who called their country the *Middle Kingdom* were convinced that China was the center of the world, and similar beliefs were held by other nations—and are still held: The British drew the Prime Meridian of longitude to run through Greenwich, near London. Europeans drew maps of the world with Europe at the center, Americans with the New World at the center.

It is interesting to note that the Romans shared the Greek belief that the northern barbarians (particularly the Germans and the inhabitants of the British Isles) were incapable of ever being civilized. And not only did they feel that the people were inferior but, perhaps because the Romans lived near the warm Mediterranean, they felt that the climate of places such as Britain was just too cold, foggy and damp for civilization ever to take root.

This last assumption of the Romans—about the effects of climate upon the capacity for civilization—is in itself typical of ethnocentric thinking. Romans, coming from a warm climate, were uncomfortable in the colder north, so they assumed that everyone must be. Much later, Europeans from the north, who found the tropics uncomfortably hot, assumed in exactly the same way that Africans and other peoples of the equatorial regions were excluded from participating in civilization because the hot climate sapped their mental energy! Had the Europeans attended the debates among the scholars at Timbuktu, a cultural and commercial center in western Africa as early as the fourteenth century, they might not have been so sure of this.

DIFFERENT = INFERIOR

As we mentioned earlier, a typical ethnocentric reaction is to assume that because people are different in appearance they are therefore inferior, or at least have something wrong with them. The dark-skinned inhabitants of New Guinea were convinced that light-skinned Europeans, when the two first came into contact, were either ghosts or at least had been dead for quite a while and had lost their skin color. Europeans claim to find the expressions on the faces of Chinese and Japanese inscrutable or mysterious, while the long nose

Two young Ethiopian technicians, one with wavy hair and the other with very curly hair. *United Nations.*

of the European is equally peculiar to the Asiatic. Similarly, throughout European history, tall northern Europeans tended to refer to smaller southern Europeans as weak and womanish, as poor fighters. Southern Europeans tended to consider northerners big, hulking, stupid brutes. There is of course no evidence that any of these characterizations was accurate.

It is interesting, however, to see how frequently enthnocentric characterizations of appearance creep into even the most scholarly and scientific of approaches. Haeckel, whom we mentioned earlier, termed the tightly curled hair of Africans (and others) *ulotrichi* ("woolly hair") by analogy with sheep. Yet such hair is as human as any other, and no more like that of a sheep than straight human hair is like that of a yak. Topinard, you will remember, said that Europeans had leptorrhine noses, a term that can be translated as "narrow" or "fine." Topinard was, of course, a European. Even today, it is not uncommon to find writers describing the "coarse" features of Africans, and noting that a few Africans appear to have "fine" features—by which they mean, of course, similar to Europeans.

Explaining Facts Away

As we saw in the case of the Greeks, ethnocentric assumptions may sometimes have to account for the fact that some of the *they* appear to be superior in some respects to *we*. The Persians and the Egyptians, for example, had built remarkable empires. The Greeks, however, preferred to believe that barbarians in the Persian and Egyptian empires were not as proud and independent as Greeks, whatever their achievements, and that made the Greeks feel better. They stopped worrying about the matter after the Greeks, under Alexander and his generals, conquered Persia and Egypt. Didn't that prove the Greeks were superior?

It is always hard to argue with soldiers who have just conquered your people, when they claim to be superior; and they, of course, are likely to pay no attention to any argument you can think up. Conquest is usually offered as self-evident proof of superiority—and has been from ancient Greece, through ancient Rome, to the very present. The only trouble is that, given enough time, conquerors tend to be conquered by someone else, who in turn fall victim to still other conquerors. One solution, and it has been offered seriously, is that the conquerors were in fact superior in the days they were conquering, but they allowed themselves to be weakened and spoiled in some way or ways, and so fell before other superior types. Lest you be tempted by the "logic" of the argument, keep in mind the distinction between a strong nation and a biologically superior people. Why should the first be evidence of the second? Perhaps the first is just larger, or spends more on armaments.

It is not clear how Europeans felt about Huns, Arabs, Moors, Turks, Mongols, and others who ravaged the subcontinent during the centuries between the fall of Rome and the final emergence of European countries as world powers. Certainly, Marco Polo and other travelers had nothing but awe and admiration for the Chinese and other civilizations they visited. The Portuguese and other Europeans, including the British, sent emissaries to beg trading rights and other favors of the haughty Great Moghul, ruler of India, when the Europeans first came into contact with this flourishing, powerful kingdom. Later, of course, when the Moghul Empire crumbled before the European cannons, some European writers claimed that the hot climate of India prevented the Indians from being good fighters.

Following hard upon Columbus, Spanish explorers moved into the New World. The peaceful inhabitants of Caribbean Islands such as Hispaniola (the present island of Haiti and the Dominican Republic) were harshly enslaved and put to work in the mines and on the plantations of the Spanish conquerors. The Indians died by the tens of thousands. Early in the sixteenth century, a Spanish priest and missionary among the Indians, Bartolome de las Casas, pleaded for the protection of the Indians and their release from their misery. He argued that they were simple, savage people who were unaccustomed to the demands of "civilized" agriculture, mining and industry and could not adapt to such things. If the Spanish required slave labor, de las Casas argued, let them seek a stronger, more advanced people as a source, capable of adjusting to the hard work demanded. He suggested that Africans were such a people and could be imported as slaves. His ideas were accepted (not so much out of pity for the Indians, but out of necessity—most of the Indians of the Caribbean, including the entire population of Hispaniola, had died or had been killed), and large numbers of Africans were brought to the New World, first by the Spanish and then by other European colonists.

This unfortunate aspect of American history has its place here because it points to the feeling of de las Casas and other Spaniards that the people of western Africa were industrious, sturdy farming folk, intelligent and hardy enough to work under the harsh conditions of colonial plantations. It was only much later, and as a partial excuse for slavery, that the myth arose that the ancestors of African slaves were cannibal hunters from the Congo jungle. Had they been, they would have been no more use to the plantation owners than the original American Indians.

Thus, as the African was forced into slavery, justification of his enslavement was sought. That he was a "jungle cannibal" was one justification, that he was a "son of Ham," condemned according to the Bible to be forever "a drawer of water and a hewer of wood" was another. Still another justification was that the African, given his climate, his appearance, and so on, was basically inferior and therefore could have no better fate than to be the slave of a member of a superior race, who would care for him. Ethnocentrism begins to shade into racism.

Ethnocentrism does not necessarily imply racism. Ethnocentrism is merely the assumption that *we* are better than *they,* an assumption held by most people in the world about their neighbors. All peoples tend to be ethnocentric. But to believe in one's superiority is one thing; to attempt to prove it, by using the findings of science, is something else. This occurred in Europe in the nineteenth century, and was to produce modern racism.

What were the ideas being introduced to the world by science in the past two or three centuries that could be picked up and used by racists? This question brings us to the next chapter.

5

Language and Race

Science is a term that has come to mean many things to many people. A favorite—and very unfortunate—use of the term in recent years has been that of a ruling, even godlike, power. "You can't argue with *science!*" crows the ignorant person, hoping to win his argument. Of course you can; that is the whole point of scientific investigation.

"The scientific method," as first proposed in the thirteenth century by the philosopher—and, many claim, the father of modern science—Roger Bacon, is a technique for investigating and understanding the natural world. Over the centuries, the method has been improved and used to investigate phenomena perhaps beyond the imaginings of Bacon. But the technique remains basically the same: Study and record carefully the matter of interest to you. Don't assume anything—take note of everything, even if it seems unimportant at the time. After sufficient study, try to develop an explanation or *hypothesis* that seems to cover the facts.

This much has been done by intelligent people everywhere in the world, and throughout man's history. Aristotle, the great Greek philosopher, for example, noted that if you leave a piece of meat in the sun it will rot, maggots will appear in it, and eventually the maggots will turn into flies. He thereupon suggested the hypothesis that the action of rotting produced maggots—in other words, that living things came out of dead meat. The term used for the idea was *spontaneous generation.*

Spontaneous generation is a perfectly good hypothesis. It doesn't happen to be correct in this particular case, of course, but many first efforts at explanation are wrong.* The trouble is that no effort was made at testing it, in Aristotle's time or for the next two thousand years. Everyone knew Aristotle was a very brilliant man, so they accepted his explanation and taught the principle of spontaneous generation of life in the schools.

The scientific method, however, requires that once an hypothesis is put forward, it must be tested. In the seventeenth century, Francesco Redi, an early Italian scientist, conducted some experiments to test the notion of spontaneous generation. In essence, he put some pieces of rotting meat in three containers; he left the top of one container uncovered, covered the second with thin gauze, and covered the third container with a piece of glass. After a period of time, he examined the containers. The meat in the first was swarming with maggots (the small, worm-like larvae of an insect such as the housefly). There were no maggots in the second, but there were tiny white specks on the gauze covering it. He took these to be eggs, since some had hatched into maggots. There was nothing in the third container (apart from rotting meat) and only a few maggots on the glass covering it. He concluded that maggots were not spontaneously generated in rotting meat, but came from eggs that had been laid on the meat, presumably by the flies he had seen hovering about the containers.

Redi's experiment was redone in different ways until Louis Pasteur, the great French scientist, finally laid the notion of spontaneous generation to rest at the end of the nineteenth century. However, if *you* are still not satisfied, by all means check it out for yourself with three pieces of meat, three containers, gauze, and glass!

For that is the most important part of the scientific method. Anyone may offer an hypothesis to explain some aspect of nature. The hypothesis, however, must not only fit all the facts presently known, but it must be capable of being tested by other investigators. That means there must be a way of proving it wrong—if it is wrong. If the explanation cannot be tested in any way, then—right or wrong—it is not acceptable to scientists. That doesn't mean that they

* There is a new version of spontaneous generation, called *abiogenesis* —the arising of *primitive* life forms from non-living things—that is scientifically sound.

reject it; they simply cannot work with it until they find a way to test it.

When an hypothesis has been tested again and again, and more and more evidence is accumulated and all goes to support the hypothesis, then it becomes widely accepted. It is usually then termed a *theory*. To call something a scientific theory does not mean that everyone believes it to be the absolute and final truth; nor does it mean, necessarily, that anyone does have doubts about it. It is simply the best explanation, everyone agrees, that can be offered. It has been tested, and every new bit of evidence confirms and supports it. It would be thrown out, of course, if new evidence is found that contradicts it, and if a better explanation is offered. Until then, it is the best explanation that students of the problem have been able to find. As Albert Einstein put it when discussing his theory of relativity: "No amount of experimentation can prove me right. But a single experiment at any time can prove me wrong."

The value of the scientific approach lies in the tremendous increase in knowledge and understanding it has brought to mankind. Mistakes have been made, incorrect explanations have often been put forth, but since no explanation is sacred to science, with continual re-testing and re-study, the errors are corrected.

While the knowledge acquired by man about the natural world in the past few centuries is enormous and would take volumes even to mention briefly, we are concerned here only with certain new discoveries and new ways of understanding man and nature which were of particular interest to the founders of modern racism.

One such discovery had to do with the relationships between languages, and another with the relationships between life forms. The second, which we cover in the next chapter, will be relatively familiar to you. The first will not, and will seem difficult. But bear with us; the ideas are important to our discussion. Adolf Hitler, for example, caused untold suffering in the world, claiming all the while that he was defending the "purity" of the Aryan super-race. Where did this word "Aryan" come from? We are going to show how he, and other racists, can take a perfectly sound scientific investigation and twist it to their own ends.

The Role of Linguistics

Modern linguistics (the study of language) is often said to begin with the findings of Sir William Jones, at the end of the eighteenth century. Other language specialists—as for example grammarians—

had studied particular languages over many centuries. The very idea of rules of grammar goes back to ancient India, many thousands of years ago. What Sir William, a brilliant British scholar and jurist, proposed had to do with an entirely different aspect of language.

If people who speak the same language are separated for a time, they will often develop differences in the way they speak that language. These variations are called *dialects*. A well-known example is the English spoken by the people in various parts of the United States, such as New England, the South and the Midwest.

If the separation is long enough and complete enough, the dialects may eventually evolve into completely different languages, as Latin gave rise to the Romance languages: French, Spanish, Italian, Portuguese, Romanian, and others. Obviously, however, there will be similarities in certain words, which will show the ancestral relationships.

While serving in Bengal, India, as a judge (this was shortly after the British conquest of Bengal), Jones became interested in the similarity of many Indian words to English and other European words, similarities that had puzzled other Europeans interested in Indian languages. The Bengali word for father, for example, is *pita* and the word for mother is *mata*. These reminded him of the Latin equivalents, *pater* and *mater* (and, for that matter, of most words in European languages for mother and father). Jones was convinced that, just as the Romance languages are originally derived from Latin, so many of the languages spoken in northern India were derived from an ancient language called *Sanskrit*. (Although Sanskrit is no longer spoken, it is still preserved as a holy language by Indians, just as Latin is preserved by Europeans.) More importantly, he was convinced that, in turn, Sanskrit, Latin, Greek, the ancestors of modern Germanic and Slavic languages, ancient Persian, and many other languages were once sister tongues (as the Romance languages are today) and were descended from a single original ancestral language, spoken in even earlier times.

Beginning with the work of Sir William, linguists in Europe studied the problem throughout the nineteenth century (and continue to do so today), and eventually were able to demonstrate the actual relationships of the languages that came to be known as the *Indo-Germanic* or *Indo-European* family of languages.

An important contribution was made by Jacob Ludwig Karl Grimm, who, with his brother Wilhelm Karl Grimm, is remembered for having written *Grimm's Fairy Tales*. Early in the nineteenth century, Jacob Grimm developed what has come to be called *Grimm's Law*. When speakers of two different dialects of one language separate, he demonstrated, and the two dialects become different languages, certain *sound shifts* (changes) take place. English and German, for example, are related, but in many words that begin with v in German (such as *vater,* meaning "father") the equivalent English word begins with f (as in father). In Latin, on the other hand, the equivalent sound would be p (as in *pater*). There is, then, according to Grimm's Law a regular, or constant patterning to the shift of sounds as languages change. It is possible to predict what the shift will be in certain cases, and—if the predictions hold up—to demonstrate by them that the languages are related. Remember how the scientific method works? Offer an hypothesis (these two languages are related) that can be tested (if I am right, you will find that *this* sound corresponds to *that* sound in the other language). If the tests hold up, and more and more evidence comes in to confirm your hypothesis, then your explanation will be accepted.

One Ancestral Language

It is now generally accepted, therefore, that there is in fact an Indo-European family of languages. There are still questions about the exact relationships, particularly as we go back further and further in time. However, by using the principle of sound shift it is possible, sometimes, to reconstruct the original word from which all the corresponding words in the daughter language are descended. English, German, Dutch, Norwegian, Swedish, Icelandic, ancient Gothic and a number of other languages have all been found to be descended from one ancestral language. Unfortunately, we have no written or other record of that language—we don't even know what it was called. We call it *proto-Germanic* (the prefix *proto-* means "earliest form of") which is usually abbreviated to *Germanic (* = proto-). Thus, the English word *good* is related to such words as *gut* (German), *goed* (Danish), *godhr* (Icelandic), *goths* (Gothic)—and by using the rules of sound shift, it is possible to reconstruct the original form, in *Germanic, from which all are descended: *gath. (We put in the asterisk because it is a reconstructed word; and of course we cannot be absolutely certain it is correct until we find it written down somewhere.) In the same way, as mentioned earlier, all the Romance languages descend from a common ancestor, *Romance (or Latin, since we know its name); further, Latin and *its* sister languages (none of them now spoken, but there are some traces of them in ancient Roman manuscripts) are descended from *Italic; Russian, Polish, Czech and other Slavic languages are descended from *Slavic. In Asia, ancient Persian and Sanskrit, along with other languages, are descended from *Indo-Iranian. *All* of these proto-languages, along with many others, including the ancient form of Greek, are descended from *Indo-European. *Indo-European appears to have been spoken, somewhere around five to six thousand years ago, in the region north and east of the Black Sea in what is today southern Russia.

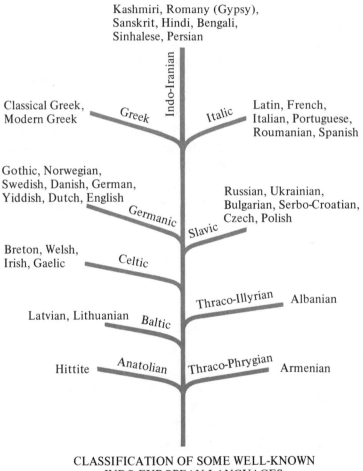

CLASSIFICATION OF SOME WELL-KNOWN INDO-EUROPEAN LANGUAGES

Derived from a table of "Language Families of the Old World" in the Columbia Encyclopedia, Columbia University Press, 1963. Placement on tree is alphabetical, and does not indicate age.

Linguists have since discovered many other great families of languages, spoken by millions of people. There is the Afro-Asiatic family, including Arabic and Hebrew; the Niger-Congo family, which includes Swahili, the Bantu languages, and many others in Africa; the Malayo-Polynesian family, including languages from areas as far apart as Hawaii and Madagascar; the Sino-Tibetan family, which includes Chinese; and so on and on. But Indo-European was the first family of languages to be charted, and it was of course of intense interest to Europeans, who were after all studying the family tree of their own languages.

These studies seemed to conjure up a very romantic, a very exciting picture. Somewhere back in the dawn of time, the ancestors of the Indo-European-speaking peoples moved out onto the arena of the world, colonizing and conquering as they went. These ancestors, speaking the dialects of the ancestral *Indo-European that were to become in time Latin, Greek, Russian, Sanskrit, and many other tongues, spread over an enormous area of Europe and Asia—from Ireland and Scandinavia in the west and north down through the Mediterranean, across the Middle East to Persia and into the heart of India. In all these places there were other languages, spoken by other peoples. Just as the other nations fell before the hardier newcomers, so—it was agreed—their languages crumbled and disappeared before the strong new Indo-European tongues. In the previous chapter it was noted that conquest is usually considered self-evident proof of superiority. Well, what greater conquest could be pointed to than the fantastic spread of Indo-European languages and their speakers? "Obviously" the speakers were superior to the men they conquered, and the languages to the ones they displaced.

A SUPERIOR PEOPLE?

What did these early speakers of Indo-European languages look like, many wondered, and what did they call themselves? Unfortunately, there were no signs or records to indicate that the earliest wanderers had writing. They left no descriptions of themselves, and no pictures. It is only hundreds of years later—perhaps even a thousand or more—that their descendants in Greece, Rome, Persia and India acquired the art of writing and left records for others to find. When there are no records, imagination can have free rein. The scholars who were studying the Indo-European languages and their speakers were in large measure German (the earlier name for the family of languages, we have seen, was Indo-German), and much of the speculation about appearance seems to have originated in Germany. It was popularly believed that the earliest speakers of *Indo-European must have been a handsome, hardy, warlike people. For northern Europeans the best example of such a people were the Vikings: tall, blond, blue-eyed.

It is customary for people to portray the past in familiar terms. In Italian paintings of the Middle Ages, biblical scenes and cities are portrayed as Italian in dress, architecture and appearance. In Holland, on the other hand, biblical personages resemble Dutch townsmen. Gautama Buddha, founder of Buddhism, was born in India, but the Japanese Buddhists portray him as Japanese. It is perfectly understandable, therefore, that northern Europeans imagined that the ancestors of all Indo-European speakers looked like northern Europeans.

It is equally understandable—but particularly important for our understanding of the development of racial ideas—that they equated the spread of the languages with superiority. Not only was it popularly believed that the original *Aryans* (according to the oldest documents in India, this is what the speakers of Sanskrit called themselves) were tall and fair, but that they were superior in every way to the peoples they conquered. It was an easy jump to extend this to all the ancient speakers of the Indo-European proto-languages.

Now, it was known of course that civilization was present in most of Europe and Asia in the regions over-run by Indo-Europeans before the coming of the new languages. Before the Greek languages arrived, for example, the Cretans had achieved a high civilization; the Persians built upon the ruins of Babylonian, Assyrian and Sumerian cities. Perhaps unconsciously, therefore, people seemed to turn to the ancient Greek solution to such a question: as we have seen, the Greeks recognized the high attainments of some "barbarians"—but denied them the full qualities accorded to Greeks. In the same way, many people believed that pre-Indo-European peoples (that is, whoever occupied territory before the coming of Indo-European speakers) were able to achieve some of the steps leading to civilization, but that *true* civilization, *high* civilization, had to await the newcomers. Only with their energy, their ability to think rationally (a characteristic of their languages, it was believed), and their capacity to organize, could civilization as we know it today come into existence.

Thus, we see how the discovery of the relationship of a group of languages scattered over Europe and Asia led to the belief that there was once an ancestral people (or peoples), speaking dialects of a language family superior to all other languages, and themselves intrinsically superior to the peoples they conquered and replaced. Let us emphasize that the evidence for the relationship of the languages was good and was continually buttressed by further work. But how do you prove that a language is superior to another? And how do you determine the color of the eyes of someone so long dead that hardly a scrap of his bone remains? Even more: how can you demonstrate whether or not present speakers of a language are actually *biological* descendants of those who spoke it thousands of years ago? After all, people learn new languages, which then replace the old. Arabic has crowded out older languages throughout the territories of Islam; but we know that the present speakers of Arabic are not all descended from the original Arabian conquerers, who brought with them both a new religion and a new language and passed both on to many other peoples. And many Americans, though descendants of immigrants from all over the world, speak the same English language as that spoken by the descendants of the original immigrants from England.

The linguistic research on the relations between languages in the Indo-European family represented scientific investigation. The other notions were simply popular fancies representing what people would like to believe about their ancestors, with little or no factual evidence to support them.

6

Progress, Evolution—and Race

As we noted in the last chapter, there was a second discovery of particular interest to those who were eventually to develop the ideas of modern racism. This was the discovery of the relationships between life forms.

The credit for this work usually goes to the famous British naturalist, Charles Robert Darwin (1809–1882), who presented his ideas to the world in 1859, in his book *The Origin of Species* and in a later book, *The Descent of Man* (1871). It should be noted, however, that the same discovery was in fact made independently and simultaneously by another British naturalist, Alfred Russel Wallace. In 1858, before the publication of *The Origin of Species,* Darwin and Wallace presented a joint paper on their discoveries before a scientific organization. This is worth remembering not merely to assure Wallace of proper credit, but because it points to something important about the nature of scientific discoveries. Such discoveries, however brilliant, are built upon the work of other scientists who went before. "I stood on the shoulders of giants," was the way Isaac Newton explained his own great discoveries. And in the same way, biological science had progressed to the point, in the mid-nineteenth century, where someone—Darwin, Wallace, or someone else with a perceptive mind—could carry it one more step.

Darwin is given most of the credit because of the great mass of evidence he presented to support his ideas, evidence that had been collected and mulled over for a period of many years. Wallace, on the other hand, completed his presentation within a few days after the idea had become clear in his mind.

In the years 1831–1836, the young Charles Darwin traveled on a world cruise, a scientific exploration on the good ship *Beagle*. As a naturalist dutifully following in the footsteps of Linnaeus, Darwin carefully recorded and catalogued all the new varieties of birds and animals discovered on the voyage. As he worked, however, something began to trouble him. For example—in the Galápagos, a group of islands some six hundred miles off the west coast of South America, he noted many varieties of birds and animals. Among them were many species of finches, most of which were not to be found on the mainland or anywhere else in the world.

The beaks of Darwin's Galapagos finches showing adaptations to each finch's eating habits.

If, as everyone believed, all the life forms in the world remained unchanging since the time of the Creation, would it not be reasonable to expect that, on isolated islands such as the Galápagos, he would find only a few representatives of species found elsewhere in larger numbers? After all, how many birds or animals could have made their way to the islands? Thus, there might be many varieties of finches in the world, and of them perhaps representatives of one or two might be found in the Galápagos. *That* would make sense. Instead, however, he found a number of varieties in the Galápagos that were not to be seen anywhere else! Was it possible that, since the Creation, they had lived—unchanging—in the Galápagos alone?

A very different idea occurred to Darwin. Suppose species were not fixed for all time, but were capable of change. In that case, what he had noted in the Galápagos and elsewhere would make sense. Here is how he reasoned. A few finches, members of some species of finch on the mainland, had found their way to the Galápagos and had survived and had many offspring. Over time, and thanks to good conditions, their descendants had given rise to many new varieties, which continued to live on the islands. This could explain why there were no representatives of these new species of birds anywhere else in the world. And if this were true, he argued to himself, then perhaps it was true of other species—perhaps of all life forms! Perhaps, when naturalists noted (following Linnaeus) that a number of species belonged to one genus, what it meant was that they were all descended from one ancestral species. And if genera could be classed together, would not that mean that, ultimately, they too went back to *one single* ancestral species? Perhaps even a *phylum*—a major division of life—ultimately went back to one single species! Who knew; perhaps *all* life went back to one primeval form.

Darwin, as you can imagine, was dazzled by the implications of his new hypothesis. He knew he must gather more evidence, and see whether his new findings tended to support his hypothesis or to weaken it. Carefully, over the years of the voyage and the years following it, he studied species and genera from all over the world. The conclusion seemed inescapable: closely related species, of any animal or plant, were descendants of one original ancestral species. The ancestral species (like a proto-language) could often be reconstructed or envisioned as the one from which the entire genus had come. In the same way, genera could, in their turn, be traced back to a single ancestral species. Linnaeus' classification of living forms turned out to be something much more than even that great man had imagined: it represented the *family tree* of life, with twigs (species) going back to branches (genera) and all the branches ultimately going back to one trunk—from which all life forms originated.

A popular cartoon during the time of controversy over Darwinism. The caption reads RETURN OF THE FOREFATHER. MR. G-G-G-G-O-O-O-O-Rilla. *The Bettmann Archive.*

Yes, *all* life forms. For Darwin had concluded that if all species had originated in this way (deriving and changing from some previous species), then—since *man* belonged to a species—man, too, derived from some earlier form. And since humans and apes obviously resembled each other, then man and the apes came originally from some ancestral (at that time unknown) species common to them all.

Understandably, there was much confusion and misinformation at first. Indeed there still is. One Victorian lady was utterly devastated by the idea—which Darwin did *not* suggest—that she was descended from the gorilla. "Please," she begged her informant, "don't let it get around."

But even the correct idea, that both man and apes derived from an earlier, different form, was most disturbing. For it was totally at variance with the common belief that man had been created a perfect being, and in his present form. Even the Bible said so. How then could he be descended from some apelike creature? Before we go further into the arguments, and discoveries, that were generated by this problem, however, let us consider two other problems of concern to Darwin.

The first question was *why* and the second question was *how: Why* did one ancestral species change over time into a number of descendant species? *How* did such a change take place?

NATURAL SELECTION

Darwin found the answer to the first; it was perhaps the most important part of his contribution to science. The answer to the second question eluded him. It had to await further scientific discoveries.

For Darwin, the question as to why speciation (spee–she–ay–shun: the development of new species from one ancestral one) took place brought him back to the finches of the Galápagos. Why, he asked himself, did one species of finch from the mainland of South America, when it reached the Galápagos, give rise over time to many new species? As part of the same question, why didn't it happen to the ancestral species back home on the mainland?

Darwin noted that birds have many ways of acquiring food, but that each species of birds has its particular or favorite way. Some birds live on flying insects, which they snap out of the air. Others, such as woodpeckers, bore for insects and their young under the bark of trees. Sea gulls go after fish, while vultures eat the rotting remains of dead animals, and hummingbirds sip the nectar of flowers. Each variety, in other words, occupies its own slot or *niche* (meaning a hole or recess in a wall: hence the position occupied by an organism in its environment), in which it can acquire its own food in its own way. Obviously, it is difficult for one variety to move to another, already-occupied, niche: could a hummingbird or a woodpecker compete successfully with a vulture?

But, suppose the other niches are *not* occupied? We return with Darwin to the case of the Galápagos finches: if a few finches from the mainland found their way to the islands, and if there were hardly any other birds there, were there not many empty niches to be occupied? As Darwin saw it, the newly arrived finches, with few enemies and much food available, multiplied quickly. After a time, specialization took place: some of the descendants of the original finches specialized in catching flying insects, some in boring under bark, some in eating seeds, and so on down the line. In the beginning, there was more than enough food for all; but as the total bird population increased there was increasing competition for the food resources of the islands. In the competition, some showed themselves better at one thing, some at another. The beaks of the Galápagos finches particularly show the specialization that took place; for example, one species has a short hard beak, another a long beak.

Darwin concluded, therefore, that life forms compete with each other for survival in a particular niche. In each species, *natural selection* takes place: those members of the species with the best ability to survive *do* survive. They live longer and have more off-spring (children), while those with less ability to survive die more quickly and have fewer offspring. Each generation, therefore, of every life form represents a *selection* of those in the previous generation; it represents those who lived long enough to have offspring, and not those who died early or without leaving descendants. If there is competition for food, it means that there is not enough food for all—some will starve to death. If a longer, or harder, beak can make the difference, then the next generation will be descended from those who survived—because they had longer or harder beaks, and the same will be true of the next generation, and the next, and the next. If longer beaks are helpful for individual survival, then, over enough time a species will probably develop with longer and longer beaks. But if there are a number of niches, and the requirements for survival are different for each niche, then by natural selection and specialization, from the one ancestral species many new species will develop, each different from the others.

On the mainland, on the other hand, there were other birds already occupying the different niches, and so the finches could not, by natural selection, differentiate and specialize.

EVOLUTION

Darwin therefore concluded that all life forms were constantly changing, or—as he put it—*evolving*. For it was not simply aimless change, but *evolution*. Through the process of natural selection, Darwin felt, all species were changing in the direction of better adaptation; better specialization for whatever were the requirements of their way of life. Some were evolving into better hunters, while others were becoming fleeter of foot and so better able to escape from hunters. Some were evolving into better swimmers, others into better flyers. Sometimes, moreover, a life form would successfully invade the territory of another; the whale and the seal were originally land animals who have, by natural selection, adapted to life in the sea. For Darwin, then, all life was fated to continuing competition for survival, and therefore to continuing evolution by natural selection.

Natural selection, therefore, explained *why* speciation took place. As we have noted, however, the explanation of *how* change took place was beyond the science of Darwin's time. Why do children look like their parents—and, sometimes, not like them? Why do the offspring of horned animals have horns? And why, occasionally, is one born *without* horns? How are the traits of the parents passed on to the children? And why, occasionally, are children born with traits that neither of the parents have?

In Darwin's time, people believed that children inherited their "blood" from parents, and that a person's blood carried the traits that made him look and act the way he did. According to this belief, the blood of two parents mingled and the offspring was a "mixture" of the two parents. If a trait appeared in the offspring that was not present in either parent, it might be a throwback to some distant ancestor. Nobody understood exactly how this could happen, nor could they explain how something entirely new might appear. *Heredity* (the means by which biological traits are passed on) was, as yet, hardly understood at all.

There were many other areas of ignorance in Darwin's time, and many other questions as yet unanswered. If, as Darwin claimed, all life forms were descended from older forms, where was the evidence of the older forms? How long did speciation take? How old was the earth?

At the beginning of the nineteenth century, the French naturalist Georges Cuvier (1769–1832) had begun the reconstruction of dinosaur fossils, and by the end of the century physicists and geologists were in agreement that the earth must be at least a few million years old. But man's knowledge of ancient life on earth was still very much in its infancy. And, in the matter of the biggest argument started by Darwin's theory of evolution—that man, himself, had evolved from some earlier, simpler form of life—there was as yet hardly any generally accepted evidence at all.

With an absence of evidence, such a notion could be roundly attacked. And it was, particularly by leaders of many religious groups, who considered it a violation of Biblical teaching. Some objectors found it necessary to challenge the entire idea of evolution. Others were willing to accept it for all other life forms—as long as man was excluded.

For there was much about the concept of evolution that was quite acceptable to nineteenth century European thought (the descent of man from an ape-like creature excepted!). The nineteenth century, after all, was a time of rapid scientific change, and of increasing European control of more and more of the rest of the world. Europeans believed in "progress"—that the world was getting to be a better and better place—and this fitted in very well with the idea of evolution.

Even more than that, the concept of evolution—as a philosophical idea, not as a biological process—was being presented in Europe at the same time as Darwin was developing his ideas. The writer mainly responsible was Herbert Spencer (1820–1903). Spencer was a British philosopher who argued that change (in the direction of progress) was characteristic of the entire universe; everything changed, became more complex, more differentiated, more specialized. This was true, he said, of the inanimate (nonliving) physical universe; it was true of life forms (he supported Darwin enthusiastically); and it was true of human society. Change, competition, progress seemed to him basic principles of the universe. Spencer, in fact, was the first to use the expression *survival of the fittest*—and Darwin apparently liked it so much that he used it himself. Indeed, the concept of natural selection has come, in many minds, to mean the same thing.

Actually, as we have seen, natural selection means something very different. It refers to the fact that any one generation is going to be represented unequally in the next generation. Some members of the first generation will have no children, some will have few children, some will have many children. The same thing will be true of the next generation, and of the next. And that is all.

Doesn't natural selection mean survival of the fittest? No. The romantic picture, in the nineteenth century, might be represented by two male gorillas fighting for a lady gorilla. The biggest, toughest fighter kills his opponent and marries the lady gorilla, passing his fighting qualities on to his children. But, from the point of view of natural selection, it doesn't matter which is the better fighter; if they both kill each other and some sneaking, cowardly little gorilla runs off with the female, then *he* makes a contribution to the next generation, and neither of the two tough fighters do. Does that make him the fittest? Yes, if we define fittest as the one having the most children.

But, as the term is popularly used, it implies the strongest or noblest or most deserving—and the expression survival of the fittest, as it was generally used in the nineteenth century, implied that the best and toughest competitor would—and *should*—win. This is why such expressions as *survival of the fittest, law of the jungle, rule of fang and claw,* and so on are no longer used in the study of biological evolution; natural selection is clearer and more accurate.

Those in the nineteenth century, however, who were interested in *social* evolution (the evolution of human behavior) , and who drew their ideas from Spencer and Darwin and applied them to the study of society, often preferred the expression *survival of the fittest.* The concepts of *biological* evolution and *social* evolution turned out to lead in very different directions.

SOCIAL VS. BIOLOGICAL EVOLUTION

Biological evolution led men to the scientific investigation of the relationship of living forms, of the nature of change and of adaptation to environment. With the discoveries in the field of genetics, Darwin's principle of natural selection took on new and greater significance, just as with Darwin's discoveries Linnaeus' classifications took on greater significance. The theory of biological evolution, buttressed by more and more evidence, came to be more and more understood and accepted by scholars, and it took its rightful place in the ever growing pyramid of knowledge.

Social evolution was a different matter, however. Based as it was on the princple of "survival of the fittest," it appealed to the ethnocentric urges of mankind. Did Europe not rule the world? Did that not prove that Europeans were the fittest of all mankind? And if they were the fittest did they not have a *right*—a *duty*—under the laws of the universe to so rule?

Evolution may in fact take place in society as well as biology. There is evidence that it does. But here we are concerned only with the above special nineteenth century approach to the question, namely that all human societies were at different levels of evolution, each frozen somehow at a given stage, while at the top was European society—the "fittest" of all, and produced therefore by the "fittest" of all human races.

We look at this idea more thoroughly in the next chapter.

7

The Birth of Modern Racism

The nineteenth century, particularly for people living in Europe, was a time of great change and stirring events. European nations, such as England, France, Holland and others, were consolidating their overseas empires and enormous quantities of the wealth of the world were pouring into the subcontinent. Along with scientific development, and to a great measure sparked by it, industrialization and mechanization were spreading widely. In the area of political ideas, too, there was much ferment and change.

Like the new ideas in science, the new political concepts had their roots in the centuries that had come before. One political issue in particular, which had increased in importance in the eighteenth century was the subject of much heated debate. In the Middle Ages, when Europe was younger, nations had been ruled by aristocratic nobles, with a king at the top; all of these "noblemen" claimed a divine, hereditary right to rule over "commoners." Suppose the king were cruel, or the nobles wicked. Did the common people have the right to choose new leaders? *No,* was the earlier belief; the aristocracy ruled by *divine right* and could not be challenged.

SOCIAL JUSTICE A NEW IDEA

In the seventeenth, and particularly in the eighteenth centuries, thoughtful men began to challenge this "divine right" to rule.

Towards the end of the seventeenth century, the British philosopher John Locke (1632–1704) argued that governments came into existence because men wished to live together in peace and prosperity, with justice provided for all. A nation, or state, therefore, represented a kind of *social contract* between the people who made it up, with laws and leaders intended to protect and benefit all. The implication of Locke's writings was that, if leaders and laws were cruel and unfair, then the contract was violated, and the people had the right to change the laws and select new leaders.

Locke's ideas were developed even further in the century to come, and most particularly by a French philosopher, Jean Jacques Rousseau (1712–1778). Among his most important works were two entitled, *Discours sur l'origine de l'inégalité des hommes* (*A discussion of the origin of human inequality*) and *Contrat social* (*Social contract*). Rousseau agreed with Locke that governments should provide justice for all. But he argued that most laws and governments *in the past* had come into existence to *cut down* men's rights and freedoms, and to transfer power to a few powerful men who then ruled for their own benefit over others. What was necessary, he felt, was for men *now* to declare that they were free men, unwilling any longer to be ruled for the benefit of a few nobles, and to enter into a new social contract guaranteeing freedom and equality for all.

The ideas of Locke and Rousseau influenced many other thinkers, and played important roles in two revolutions that shook the world: the American Revolution and the French Revolution. The cry of the French, as they overthrew the aristocracy and the king was: "Liberty! Equality! Fraternity!" In the Thirteen Colonies, we can detect the influence of Locke and Rousseau in the Declaration of Independence, in which Thomas Jefferson wrote:

> We hold these truths to be self-evident, that all men are created equal, that they are endowed by their Creator with certain inalienable Rights, that among these are Life, Liberty and the Pursuit of Happiness.—That to secure these rights, Governments are instituted among Men, deriving their just powers from the consent of the governed,—That whenever any Form of Government becomes destructive of these ends, it is the Right of the People to alter or abolish it, and to institute new Government, laying its foundation on such principles and organizing its powers in such form, as to them shall seem most likely to effect their Safety and Happiness.

These truths seemed self-evident to the American colonists, to the French revolutionaries, and to others in Europe who, during the next (nineteenth) century, wished to overthrow aristocratic governments and replace them with democratic republics. They certainly didn't seem self-evident to most of the kings and nobles who were losing their lands, privileges, and often their lives. Many of the nobles, of course, fought the new republicans with weapons; but some joined in the war of ideas, hoping to convince people that Locke, Rousseau, and their followers were wrong—that there were, in fact, very good reasons why commoners should continue to allow aristocrats to rule over them.

THE COMTE DE GOBINEAU

One of the most important of such aristocratic replies—important at least for the issues discussed in this book—came from the pen of Joseph Arthur, Comte (Count) de Gobineau (1816–1882). Gobineau was a French writer and diplomat who—as one can tell from his name—claimed aristocratic origins. One of his uncles was involved in a plot to restore the monarchy to France, and Gobineau himself apparently admired the good old days before the French Revolution.

His most important work was entitled *Essai sur l'inégalité des races humaines* (1853–1855), which was translated into English under the title: *Essay on the Inequality of Races*. From the title, it certainly sounds as if he intended the work to be a reply to Rousseau's famous essay of the previous century.

Gobineau raised the question of why there were mighty civilizations in some parts of the world, but only barbarism in other parts. Further, he inquired, why did some great civilizations crumble into dust, while others survived and continued? Drawing upon the knowledge available in his time (but selecting only what contributed to support his arguments!) in linguistics, archaeology, anthropology, biology and history, he developed answers for his questions.

Man, he said, was divided into three basic and separate races: the white, the yellow and the black. As we have seen earlier, even by Gobineau's time anthropologists and anatomists were no longer satisfied with this overly simple division, which did not take into account many of the variations to be seen among humans; but their worries did not trouble Gobineau. He was, after all, not an honest scientist trying to understand more clearly the world around him; he was in effect a racist who was looking for any idea, trustworthy or not, which he could use in his argument.

According to Gobineau, these three races had once been completely separate and distinctive in appearance and behavior; in other words, originally any member of any of the three races could be identified not only by his color (white, yellow, black) but also by the way he acted, and by the way his mind worked (or didn't work). Whites, he felt, were characterized as energetic, good fighters, and above all, good leaders. The yellow peoples, on the other hand, were calm and plodding, very stable and therefore hard workers, and above all, very fertile. (That is, they tended to have lots and lots of children, which was why, for Gobineau, there were so many people in such Asian countries as China and India.) For him, the blacks were the most inferior of the three (the whites of course were the most superior) and the only good quality he could see in blacks was artistic ability. Apart from that, he felt, they were simple, happy folk, who enjoyed deeply the ordinary simple pleasures of life.

Gobineau believed that the qualities of each race were carried in the blood of its members, and so were passed on to their descendants. Terrible things happened, he felt, when mixtures of blood of two races took place; worst of all, most of the qualities of the superior parent would be lost forever. Thus, for Gobineau, the worst mixture was between black and white—for the descendants of such a mixture would be people who might look white (though perhaps a little darker than the pure whites) but would have the mental characteristics of the blacks.

How did he know? Because, he said, it had already happened, with terrible results. Once, thousands of years ago, there had been a pure white race—blond, blue-eyed, tall, long-headed—the *Aryans!* Some of them had conquered India, and introduced Sanskrit and civilization. Others—the ancestors of the Greeks and Romans—had introduced Indo-European languages and civilization to Europe. But where are the tall, blond, blue-eyed Greeks and Romans today? If one visited southern Europe, he noted, one found only short, round-headed, dark-haired, swarthy-skinned people—interested in pleasure, in music and the arts. Obviously, then, the early Aryan Greeks and Romans must have made the mistake of intermarrying with blacks (Gobineau considered most of the original inhabitants of the Mediterranean area, including the Jews, to be blacks) and their descendants were inferior or degenerate types. To prove it, he pointed out that little or nothing remained in Greece or Italy of the once-glorious Greek and Roman civilizations.

Fortunately, he felt, the farther north in Europe one went, the less contact people had had with the contaminating blacks—and in the far north were still to be found examples of the pure white race: the blond, blue-eyed, tall, energetic, long-headed *Nordic,* the last remnant of the *Aryans!*

Gobineau pointed out that when Rome fell, because its people had become weakened and spoiled through intermarriage with inferior types, strong, pure Nordic Aryans moved in to replace the Romans. Germanic peoples had conquered Europe—the Goths had conquered Italy and Spain, the Angles and Saxons had invaded Britain, the Franks and Burgundians had taken over France. The only problem, according to Gobineau, was that unfortunate mixing started taking place again. Mixed and degenerate, the Goths soon disappeared from the scene in their turn, and farther north the Aryan conquerors were mixing with the degenerate inhabitants of France and Britain. There was a final wave of Aryans; Vikings conquered northern France, giving rise to the Normans, who went on to conquer England, Sicily and even Palestine.

Thus, according to Gobineau, the aristocracy of Europe, deriving from one wave or another of Nordic invaders, represented the purest, most fully Aryan, of any members of their nations. As such, therefore, they had the finest leadership qualities, and were in every way the most superior individuals. Did not the possession of such qualities, then, give them the right to rule? And, further, if the aristocrats were deposed, and government turned over to the mongrel mob, would that not spell the end of European civilization, as it had spelled the end of civilizations in the past? There was an enemy at the gate of Europe, Gobineau warned: the yellow races of Asia might lack brilliance and the other fine Aryan qualities, but they made up for it in hard work and dogged determination and—above all—in numbers. What was to be known later as the *yellow peril* was lurking at the borders, Gobineau believed, to inherit the wreckage produced by the wild ideas of equality and liberty introduced by Rousseau and others.

As you read this chapter, you may wonder why so much space is being devoted to a man whose ideas have been thoroughly discredited by scholars everywhere. The reason is that Gobineau's arguments have remarkable recuperative powers. Stamped out here, they arise someplace else, or in the *same* place, later on. True, some of his notions were discarded early; but some seem still to be held today,

OUR VISITORS.

JONATHAN. "Ah! Mister, and, pray, what can I do for you?"
JAPANESE VISITOR. "If you please, I would like to borrow a little of your light."

A European view of the Asian seeking "light" from European civilization. This cartoon appeared in nineteenth-century newspapers. *The Bettman Archive.*

even by thinking men and women. The people who hold them may never have heard of Gobineau; they might even be shocked to learn of the source of their beliefs. And often they will present the ideas as new, or at least as self-evident and unarguable.

But Gobineau's teachings are important for still another reason. As we shall soon see, they were picked up and developed by many other writers in different parts of the world, often with disastrous results.

Some of Gobineau's arguments are so transparently false—at least to us—as not to deserve comment. Other points have been touched on in previous pages. Let us now consider the idea of the blond Aryan as a superior being. (In parts of the following section, you need only substitute *white* for Aryan or Nordic to bring the discussion right into present-day society.)

It is possible that some of the early Greeks who invaded the Mediterranean world were blonde; the evidence is unclear. But by the time of the fifth century B.C., when Greek civilization began to climb to new heights, the inhabitants of Greece looked little different from the people who live there now. There is certainly no evidence that the Romans were ever tall and fair, and at the time of Rome's greatest conquests, Roman writers were describing the Germanic peoples to the north as very different from themselves (and, of course, inferior!). As for the actual Aryans—those Indo-European-speaking peoples who, according to the most ancient legends of India, moved from the deserts and mountains of the northwest down into the plains of northern India, there is every reason to believe they resembled the tan-skinned, dark-haired people who presently reside in Afghanistan and Persia. Blond, blue-eyed, tall people are found in largest numbers in northern Europe and among people who are descended from immigrants from northern Europe, and no one, not even Gobineau, has ever really tried to argue that the Aryans or, for that matter, the Greeks or the Romans came originally from Scandinavia.

Gobineau's belief that only Nordics can build and maintain great civilizations, or at least great empires, is difficult to support when examined closely. Great civilizations and empires came into existence in many places in the world without benefit of Nordic leadership. (There are still those, however, who cherish the belief that the Aztec and Inca empires of the New World owe their beginnings to the Vikings—something that most scholars today tend to reject.) The great Chinese kingdom, for example, arose and persisted for thousands of years—much longer, and much greater in size, than anything in Europe up to the nineteenth century—without any sign of Nordic or Aryan help. In Africa, too, there were powerful states, for example, Ghana and Bornu, which flourished south of the Sahara long before the rise of the great European powers. Consider the Songhai Empire around Lake Chad, which flourished at the time of Charlemagne (about 800 A.D.) and was to last far longer than his empire.

Furthermore, if only the pure Nordic type has the genius for civilization and empire, why did civilization and empire develop in *southern* Europe and southwestern Asia—and *never* (at least until comparatively recently) in northern Europe? It is true, of course, that the Roman Empire collapsed as, given enough time, all empires

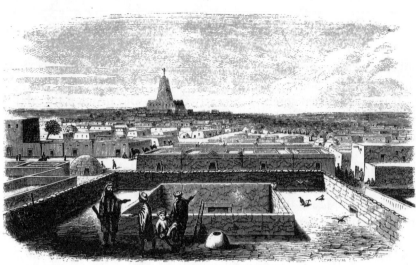

TIMBUKTU, FROM THE TERRACE OF THE TRAVELER'S HOUSE.

Engraving showing the African city, Timbuktu, as it looked more than a century ago. *A. Barth, Travels and Discoveries in North and Central Africa, Harper, 1859.*

apparently do. But the reasons for that collapse are still being debated by historians—and mixture of blood is rarely offered anymore as a reason. It is also true that, with the collapse of the Roman Empire, Germanic-speaking peoples from northern Europe moved into the vacuum and established themselves in power in many places. But there were others who moved in to carve out chunks of the Roman Empire—the Arabs, the Turks, the Huns, and so on—who could hardly be classified as Aryans!

In this book, however, we are particularly concerned with Gobineau's ideas on race. In good scientific tradition, we want to know where the evidence is to support the idea that whites are more energetic than yellows, that blacks are more artistic than whites, and so on. Most disturbing of all to us is the fact that Gobineau's entire argument rests upon the notion that mankind can be divided into three distinct and separate races: the white, the yellow and the black; we have plodded the weary road from Linnaeus to Blumenbach to Haeckel to Coon and others. All, we have seen, is confusion and uncertainty. There is, however, *one* thing we can say for sure: whatever the divisions of mankind, it is *not* divided into just three races, white, yellow and black!

Few, if any, responsible scholars, truly interested in understanding human similarities and differences, paid much attention to the writings of Joseph Arthur, Comte de Gobineau. There were, however, many others in Europe and the United States for whom Gobineau's notions were exciting and appealing. We have seen that almost any appeal to ethnocentric superiority will find interested listeners. It is said that Gobineau himself, during a visit to an island in the North Sea, was thrilled to think that he must be descended from a noble Viking from that island.

A similar feeling came over an Englishman named Houston Stewart Chamberlain (1855–1927) who went to school in Germany and decided to settle there permanently. He married a German girl (the daughter of Richard Wagner, the composer), and studied the writings of Gobineau. He became convinced that Gobineau was right, and in 1899 wrote a book, *Foundations of the Nineteenth Century*, in support of Gobineau's ideas.

Gobineau, you recall, believed that the common people of Europe had been "mongrelized" (made inferior by mixture) and that only in the aristocracy was there still a trace of Aryan superiority. Chamberlain went even further; he claimed that mongrelization had already progressed too far in France, England and other countries. Only in his adopted homeland, Germany, was there still hope for the purity of the Aryan race! The Germans, he felt were the last true descendants of the Teutons (actually, an ancient German tribal name) who, he believed, were the best and noblest of the Aryans. If the Germans could manage to preserve their racial purity and reject the ideas of equality that were destroying France and England, then his new fatherland would inherit from other faltering hands the control of Europe, and perhaps of the world.

Chamberlain's book, it may be imagined, was quite popular in Germany. It is said, for example, to have been among the favorite reading of Kaiser Wilhelm II, who ruled from 1888 to 1918.

Like Gobineau before him, Chamberlain disliked and distrusted the Jews. For one thing, as a result of the French Revolution (detested equally by Gobineau and Chamberlain), the Jews of Europe had been allowed to leave the ghettoes in which they had been imprisoned throughout the Middle Ages. Now they were free to attend the schools, wear the clothes, and engage in the activities of other Europeans. It was becoming difficult to tell who was a Jew, and who was not. In addition, Jews and non-Jews were intermarrying. Since Chamberlain, like Gobineau, believed that the Jews were an inferior, dark-skinned people originally from the Mediterranean, such intermarriages posed a terrible threat: they would mongrelize the otherwise pure Aryans!

Furthermore, Chamberlain, like Gobineau and others who believed in the rights of aristocrats, was convinced that many of the ideas of equality and liberty that had spread through Europe were started by Jews. Many Germans, including Chamberlain, rejected even Christian teachings about brotherhood of man—claiming these were Jewish ideas which had been slipped into Christianity by Jews, and must be eliminated from Nordic thinking if the pure race was to be preserved.

Twenty years after Chamberlain's book appeared, it began to influence a group of young Germans who were starting a new party, which they called the National Socialist party—and which came to be called Nazi for short. Germany had been badly defeated in the first World War; the German people were angry and hurt that they had lost, and were suffering from the effects of the war.

THE NAZIS

Adolf Hitler (1889–1945) the leader of the new Nazi party, wrote a book entitled *Mein Kampf* ("my struggle"), in which he borrowed heavily from the ideas of Houston Stewart Chamberlain. Hitler argued that the Germans were, in fact, the Aryan super-race that Chamberlain had called them. They *did* deserve to rule the world, he claimed, for they were the best fighters and would make the best leaders and rulers.

Why then had they lost the war if they were so great? Hitler claimed that the war had been lost because of Jewish treachery. The Jews, he claimed, wanted to rule the world themselves, and knew that in order to do so would have to get rid of the Germans first. Therefore, he argued, rich Jews weakened the economy of Germany. Jewish politicians sold out to the enemy. Jewish men, he believed, loved to have children by German girls, because that meant the children would be mongrelized. Worst of all, perhaps, Jews spread "Jewish" ideas of brotherhood, peace, equality, love-thy-neighbor and other undesirable thoughts.

The Nazis, under Hitler, promised to put a stop to all this. If given power, they would erase all teachings of equality and brotherhood. They would re-introduce the manly and noble Aryan virtues: Strength, power, leadership. Jews would be prevented from ever harming the German people again, and under the leadership of Adolf Hitler the new *Aryans* would go on to conquer the world, as was their proper destiny.

As a symbol of their beliefs, the Nazis chose the *swastika,* an ornamental religious design quite common in India which the Nazis believed went back to the original Aryans from whom all Indo-Europeans were supposed to be descended.

Many people in Germany and elsewhere in the world thought Hitler's ideas were silly, but there was nothing to laugh at anymore when, in 1932, Hitler and his Nazi Party came into power in Germany. Hitler did his very best to carry out his ideas, and those (as he saw them) of his teacher, Chamberlain, and his teacher's teacher, Gobineau. Young Germans were taught to consider teachings of the Bible such as "peace on Earth, good will towards men" as Jewish-inspired and to model themselves on the ancient warrior-heroes of the Teutons. Jews were forbidden to attend German schools or hold government jobs. They were particularly forbidden to marry non-Jews. Since there had been intermarriage in the past, there was a problem as to who was a Jew and who was not. It was decided that anyone who had at least one Jewish grandparent had Jewish "blood" and was to be treated like all other Jews. Thus, protected from "Jewish treachery," the Germans armed for World War II.

Still, even without "Jewish treachery" the Germans lost the war. The notion of Aryan superiority that had been first developed by Joseph Arthur, Comte de Gobineau, was apparently laid to rest in 1945. With it, however, were buried some tens of millions of the people of all the countries of Europe, victims of the war. This included almost all the Jews of Europe—some six million men, women and children.

GOBINEAU'S INFLUENCE IN THE UNITED STATES

In addition to Houston Stewart Chamberlain and the Nazis, Gobineau had other followers, particularly in the United States. The concern in the United States was not, as in Germany, with the warlike qualities Gobineau ascribed to the Aryan. Of more concern was Gobineau's assertion that any intermarriage with members of other races would invariably result in inferior offspring.

There were two sources of worry. In the nineteenth century, after the Civil War, the descendants of African slaves were freed. Did that mean, people were arguing, that they should have the same rights as citizens of European ancestry? Should they be permitted to vote, to run for office? Did they have the ability to do so? Furthermore, should the descendants of Africans and Europeans be permitted to intermarry freely, if they wished?

The second source of worry came from increasing immigration, mostly from Europe. The earliest colonists had come from England, Scotland and Ireland. By the beginning of the twentieth century, however, enormous numbers of people were pouring into the United States from other parts of Europe, particularly Italians from southern Europe and Jews and Poles from eastern Europe. Was it all right to let these newcomers in? Would they be able to participate in American democracy? What would happen if they were to intermarry with the older Americans? Gobineau seemed to provide answers to these questions.

It is difficult to say for certain that attitudes towards the American Negro (those who were known to be descended, in whole or in part, from Africans) derived solely from Gobineau. Many of his ideas were commonly held by others long before he wrote—for example, the notion that blacks were a happy folk, who loved nothing more than to sing and dance and play all day. It is fair to note, therefore, that many popularly held opinions among European-Americans about their "black" fellow-citizens, in the last quarter of the nineteenth century, were identical to the statements of Gobineau about "blacks." It was argued, particularly in the southern states (but many Northerners agreed), that people of African ancestry lacked the capacity to participate in the democratic processes; they would not know how to vote wisely, and a person of African ancestry could not serve properly if elected to office. In other words, to use Gobineau's concepts, only whites had the ability and right to govern.

Furthermore, it was widely believed that intermarriage between whites and blacks would lead to "mongrelization." Some argued that the offspring of such a "mixture of blood" would be inferior to *both* parents, but anyway almost everyone agreed the children of such a match would be inferior to the white parent.

Immediately after the Civil War, people of any ancestry were allowed to vote and to run for office. A number of men, descendants of Africans, had been elected to state offices, to the House of Representatives and to the Senate of the United States. By the late 1870s, this had come to an end, cut short by a concerted effort on the part of those who felt threatened by this turn of events. Restrictive laws were passed in many states, and accepted by the Federal Government. The wording varied, but the result was the same; few people of African descent could vote, and none was elected to office. Other laws were passed, making it a crime for people of African and European ancestry to marry. Such marriages were termed *miscegenation*. This is an interesting word for us. It was apparently coined in 1864 in the United States, and was considered better than the word it replaced: *amalgamation*. Miscegenation comes from two Latin words, *miscere* (to mix) and *genus* (we know that one!) and so it is used to mean a mixture of races.

It certainly sounds as if someone had been reading Gobineau.

So much for the threat of the black. What of the immigrant?

WHITES CAN BE INFERIOR TOO

In 1916, Madison Grant, a naturalist at the American Museum of Natural History in New York, published a book entitled, *The Passing of the Great Race*. Obviously much influenced by Gobineau, Grant explained to his readers that the world contained but one Great Race—the Nordic branch of the white* race—and that this race of blond, blue-eyed, dynamic leaders had created and maintained civilization. The black race was—as we might expect—described as the most inferior of all, incapable of achieving or keeping civilization, suitable only to perform labor for the whites. Madison Grant, however, was particularly concerned with varieties of the white race other than the Nordic. To put it simply, he argued that those people in Europe of Nordic extraction (Scandinavians, Germans, Englishmen, and so on) were most desirable to have as immigrants to the United States. Frenchmen (peace to poor old Gobineau!) were less desirable, because they came from farther south in Europe, and thus were closer to the blacks. Italians, Spaniards, Greeks and other Southern Europeans were still less desirable, of course, and Slavs (Poles, Russians and other Eastern Europeans, including Jews) were in about the same category: very undesirable.

The reason these people were so undesirable was that they might, if allowed to settle in the United States, intermarry with the Nordic population. The offspring of any marriage between a Nordic and a representative of *any* other (and therefore inferior) race would invariably resemble the non-Nordic parent, Grant insisted. He explained that Nordic blood—though superior in every other way—had one weakness: when mixed with the blood of any other race it would lose its qualities and the inferior blood would be dominant. To

* We remind the reader that words such as white, black, and Nordic should be read as if they had quotation marks around them.

prove his point, he noted that if a person with blue eyes (a character-istic of Nordics, he believed) married a person with brown eyes, their children would, in almost every case, have brown eyes. As we shall see later, Grant was right but for the wrong reasons. For the moment, let us just note that brown eyes are said by students of genetics to be *dominant* and blue eyes are said to be *recessive*. But this in no way was proof of his arguments. Nevertheless, he main-tained that the same was true of all the characteristics, mental as well as physical, of the Great Race.

We have already pointed to many of the weaknesses in Gobineau's argument, which were simply repeated by Madison Grant. His state-ments about the inheritance of eye color showed a great misunder-standing of the nature of inheritance. Even in Grant's own time, there were scholars who tried to point out his errors and mis-statements.

But people preferred to listen to Madison Grant, and not to the well-informed scientists. At least, it is known that the Congress of the United States preferred Madison Grant. He was called in as an expert advisor by the committees drawing up legislation to restrict immigration, and his ideas (or, should we say, Gobineau's?) formed the principles underlying the Immigration Acts of 1921 and 1924. Under these laws, quotas were established according to National Origin—that is, only so many people of a given nationality were to be allowed into the country each year. The quotas were set up so that the largest number of immigrants could come from Great Britain, the Scandinavian countries, and Germany. The quotas for people from southern and eastern European countries were very small. With a few exceptions, Asians and Africans were completely excluded. The 1952 Immigration and Nationality Act modified some of the provi-sions of the earlier acts but did not change the basic idea. As of this writing, the racial notions of Joseph Arthur, Comte de Gobineau, remain imbedded in the laws of the United States.

Gobineau's ideas continue to live on in other ways. Carleton Putnam, an American lawyer, in a book entitled *Race and Reason* (1961) argues strongly against integration in schools. He argues too in favor of laws preventing people of European and African ancestry from marrying each other. While he does not mention either Gobi-neau or Grant by name in his book, many of his arguments remind us of theirs. For example: "Our American Republic, with all its faults, is, together with England, the fine flower of centuries of self-discipline and experience in free government by the English speaking branch of the White race. I will not say no other branch, but I will say few other races, have ever approached this achievement, least of all the Negro" (p. 41). And: "But one thing is sure: crossing a superior with an inferior breed can only pull the superior down" (p. 59).

One may even detect what sounds like an echo of still another follower of Gobineau in Putnam's arguments. He tells us that members of certain European minority groups (unidentified by Putnam, but the names of members of the groups that he gives are Jewish names) came to America and were unhappy at "what they considered unjustified discrimination. . . ." They tried to achieve equality for themselves, he argues, "by proving that *all* races were equal in their adaptability to our white civilization" (p. 47). Jewish scholars, Putnam seems to be saying, have fooled others into believing that Negroes deserve equal treatment, in order to serve the special purposes of the Jews, and "to advance what they conceive to be the interests of their special stocks, [and] promote theories and policies which are bound to weaken the white race as a whole" (p. 48). We have heard that argument before, haven't we?

Still others have inherited the notions of Gobineau. His basic argument, remember, was that races were unequal—that members of each race shared the basic psychological character of that race, what might perhaps be called its "soul." Some disciples of Gobineau (who may not even know that they are) have simply turned his ideas around slightly, without too much violence to the basic argument. Who says, after all, that the Great Race has to be Nordic—or even that it has to be white? Anyone can play that game, and many do; their race (whichever one it may be and however they may define it) is the "Great Race" with special qualities of body and soul that characterize all its members, and to preserve those qualities members of the "Great Race" must not associate with members of other, inferior races.

But those of us who want to do more than simply make the same old ethnocentric claim—*we* are better than they—must bear in mind that *all* the claims of Gobineau and all the racists who followed after him are based upon error and ignorance: error about how many races of man there are, and what they are; and ignorance of the nature of heredity.

We must therefore continue our exploration of what is known—and what is *not* known—about the nature and variations of mankind, and the origins of man.

8

The Discovery of Genetics

We have seen that the serious students of human variation, from Linnaeus and Blumenbach onward, appeared to believe that there was some connection between a particular group and its geographical location. The tendency, in fact, was to name a group after its location (European man, African man, and so on). It is not always clear whether they meant that geography and climate could produce a particular race *once,* in the past, when the present races began, but that now all the races were fixed and unchanging—or whether immigrants from any other part of the world would in time change to resemble the race of the area.

These and other questions are unclear, and one can find statements to support almost any position in the early writings, because the early students of human variation understood little or nothing about the biological reasons for variation. They could use, in their descriptions of race, only physical traits—usually, items of appearance, such as skin color or hair shape. What caused these differences in appearance? No one could say. If the same trait appeared in two widely separated parts of the world, were the traits biologically identical (were the people related) or not? No one could say.

SIMILARITIES AND DIFFERENCES IN HUMAN BEINGS

Let us see if we can find some answers to these questions. We know that members of a species (the human species, or any other) resemble each other exactly in certain traits, but vary widely in others. All pigs without exception, for example, have hoofs at the ends of their forelegs—while all humans have hands with fingers. True, an occasional unfortunate baby, anywhere in the world, might be born without hands or fingers—but there is *no group* of humans, anywhere in the world, without hands and fingers. In other words, Blumenbach would have been wasting his time if he tried to divide the human species up into races on the basis of whether or not they had hands or hoofs; hands are found universally in the species. If some groups of humans had *tails,* that would certainly be an easy way of dividing up the species—but while an occasional baby (very rarely) is born with a tail, no human population may be characterized as having tails.

Humans vary enormously in skin color—but not at all in the presence or absence of tails. Why one, and not the other? It turns out that members of a species resemble one another *identically* in many more ways than they differ; that has to be the case, or they couldn't be members of the same species. Even different species, members of the same genus, resemble each other in very large measure; we share the same basic blood types, you will remember, with gorillas, chimpanzees and others.

The variety of human similarities and differences is indicated in this picture of the United Nations Economic Committee. *United Nations.*

Therefore, those comparatively few ways in which members of a species differ are obviously very interesting. The question of why there should be variation in those traits alone is only part of the problem. Where, in the biological construction of the creature does the source of the variation lie? If two members of the species with slightly different traits should mate and have children, will the children resemble one of the parents, or be a mixture of both? Where does a new variation come from? Suppose a baby is born with a tail. Why should it have a tail when neither of its parents did? Why doesn't its brother have a tail? If the baby grows up and has children, will they all be born with tails? Or will some of them? None?

In the nineteenth century, with all the interest in the exciting new theory of evolution, it seemed that no one could answer these questions. Charles Darwin, for example, believed that, through natural selection, variations within a species spread and gave rise to new species. Yet he had no idea where the variations came from. Up to the year 1900, in fact, no one in the world—*with one exception*—could even begin to answer these questions. There was one man who made a good beginning in answering these questions, but his work lay forgotten or unnoticed for almost forty years.

MENDEL AND HIS PEAS

Gregor Johann Mendel (1822–1884), born in Austria, decided to spend his life in religious contemplation. In 1843, he joined the monastery at Brno, (or Brunn) in what is today Czechoslovakia, and there he spent the rest of his life. The furor in scientific circles about speciation and variation reached even to the monastery at Brno, and the monk, Gregor Mendel, asked himself the same questions others were asking: why do some offspring resemble their parents, while others do not? What kind of offspring are born when parents with different traits are mated?

Mendel, however, did more than just raise questions. He decided to try to find the answers by means of experiment. Anyone who wishes may repeat his experiments and see for himself whether Mendel was right in his conclusions.

Mendel turned to the monastery garden and began his investigation with the crossbreeding of plants. He chose, for his first experiments, certain varieties of the common garden pea. In one experiment, he selected two types: one a tall variety, the other a short (dwarf) variety. All of the plants used in the experiment were selected carefully to be certain they were pure strains—that is, the tall ones would, if bred, produce *only* tall offspring, generation after generation, while the dwarf specimens would produce *only* dwarf offspring, generation after generation.

Mendel's first step was to crossbreed a tall pea-plant with a dwarf pea. He termed the two parent plants the P (for parent) generation. He then planted the seeds that resulted from the crossbreeding, and awaited results.

Mendel named the plants of the next generation the F_1 generation: the F was for the Latin word *filius,* meaning son or descendant, and the 1 meant it was the first descending generation. When Mendel examined the F_1 generation, he found that *all* the plants, without exception, were as tall as their tall parent. The same thing happened every time he crossbred tall and dwarf plants. On the basis of this evidence, he concluded that the trait tall was *dominant* in peas, while the trait dwarf was *recessive;* that is, tallness prevailed in the F_1 generation while dwarfishness seemed to disappear.

Or, Mendel asked himself, was it just in hiding somewhere? To find out, he proceeded to cross the plants of the F_1 generation with each other to see what would happen in the next, or F_2, generation. The results were fascinating. Three out of four of the F_2 plants were again as tall as their parents and their tall grandparent. *One* out of four, however, was a dwarf plant—exactly like the dwarf grandparent! Mendel had proved that recessive traits do not disappear; they just seem to go into hiding!

Mendel continued with his experiments, crossbreeding members of the F_2 generation in various ways. Again certain surprising discoveries resulted. First, he found that the F_2 dwarf, if mated with another F_2 dwarf, produced nothing but dwarf offspring in the F_3 generation, and in the F_4 generation, and so on for as long as he continued to mate them. In other words, two F_2 dwarf peas, both of them offspring of two tall F_1 peas, produced *no* tall offspring or descendants. Tallness might be dominant in peas, Mendel noted, but the recessive dwarfishness could still appear in descendants—and once two dwarf descendants were mated, they would never have a tall descendant unless one of them was mated with a tall plant.

Mendel turned to the three out of four tall plants in each F_2 generation. What kind of descendants would *they* have? After much study, he determined the following: two out of every three of the F_2 tall plants would behave just like their parents—they would have, on the average, three tall descendants and one dwarf. *One* of the three tall F_2 plants, however, would have tall descendants and *only* tall descendants from then on!

To sum up, Mendel had found that when he crossbred a pure tall pea with a pure dwarf pea, the result was offspring that were all of them tall. These, however, invariably produced out of every four offspring: *one* line that was pure dwarf, *one* line that was pure tall, and *two* lines that were exactly like the parents, and would continue to have the same mixture of offspring. Mendel's findings can be expressed in a simple diagram, as shown.

Generation

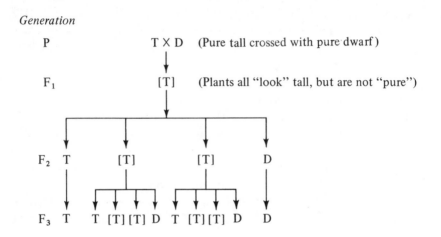

(One pure T and one pure D plus two [T]-like parents)

The diagram shows the probable results of crossing a tall pea plant T with a pure dwarf pea plant D and then crossing the plants in the F_1 generation with one another. This experiment was performed by Gregor Mendel in the mid-nineteenth century.

One thing, of course, was quite clear to Mendel as a result of these and other similar experiments. The old notion that, when parents with two different traits mated, a mingling, or mixing, of the traits took place in the offspring, was obviously false. But what new explanation, or hypothesis, could be offered to explain what he had found, and to predict what would happen in future experiments?

By Mendel's time, through the use of the microscope and other devices, biology had progressed to the point where some of the processes of reproduction were understood. It was known, for example, that while all complex organisms (most animals, including man, and most plants) were composed of many cells, reproduction took place because one special reproductive cell from each parent was able to fuse with a similar cell contributed by another parent. Such a special reproductive cell is called a *gamete* (gam'–eet). When two gametes, one from a male parent and one from a female parent, meet and fuse together, they form a new cell, called a *zygote* (zy'–goat), which then divides, and redivides, until an entire new organism is formed.

GENES—THE UNITS OF HEREDITY

Mendel concluded, therefore, that the gamete, or sex cell, produced by an individual contained some sort of controlling or directing mechanism for each trait of the new organism that was to grow out of it. It was to be many years before scientists understood clearly what this directing mechanism was, and how it worked, but a name soon developed for it: *gene* (jeen). The gene, then, is the unit of heredity, and Mendel theorized that the new zygote inherited one such unit from each parent for each trait that would appear in the adult. A gamete had only one unit (or gene) for each trait, but that was not enough to produce a new organism. Two gametes had to join together, so that a zygote was formed with a *pair* of genes for each trait, in order for a new organism to develop.

The study of *genetics* (the science of biological inheritance) has come a long way since it began with Mendel's experiments, and we now know, for example, that it can take more than one gene from a parent to affect a trait in the adult, but Mendel understood the basic facts: heredity is governed by the inheritance of an equal number of directional units from each parent, which then pair together in the zygote; and it is the new *pair* of units that determines what the new organism will look like in regard to that trait.

Mendel realized, further, that when the two parental genes join together, they may be identical (that is, for peas, both may be directives for tallness or both for dwarfishness) or the two parents may contribute two different genes. In such a case, as we have seen, Mendel noted that one directive is often dominant and the other recessive. Nevertheless, he concluded, the genes themselves do not mingle, but remain separate, and when the organism grows up and produces a sex gamete of its own, it can only contain *one gene* of the original pair. This *principle of segregation*—that genes somehow continue to maintain their separate identity in the new organism— was Mendel's hypothesis for explaining the results of his experiment.

To see how this works, let us go back to the original experiment. Mendel, you will remember, chose for his P generation two plants, one of a pure tall strain, the other of a pure dwarf strain. By pure we mean that the tall plant had inherited genes for tallness from both of its parents. In other words, we could represent the plant's genetic directives for height as: (TT) —made up of two genes for tallness. The custom is to use a capital letter, since—as Mendel discovered, tallness is dominant. The dwarf parent, of course, had two genes for dwarfishness. Since this is recessive, the custom is to represent it with the small, or lower-case, form of the same letter as is used for the dominant trait. Thus, we say that the dwarf plant's genetic directive for height was: (tt).

Each parent produced a gamete (sex cell) with only one gene for height. In other words, from a parent with the pair (TT) could come only (T) gametes, while from a cell in the dwarf parent with the pair (tt) could come only (t) gametes. The new zygote would then inherit one of each and so the F₁ generation would have a mixed pair (Tt). Since T (or tallness) is dominant, the F₁ generation would all be tall, but they would all carry the recessive gene for dwarfishness; and, according to Mendel's principle of segregation, the gene would keep its separate identity.

Now let us see what happens when we mate two members of the F₁ generation, each with a mixed pair of genes for height, (Tt). Each parent, let us remember, produces gametes which have only *one* of the pair of parental genes. Thus, from each F₁ parent, the gamete

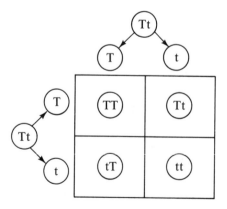

A Mendelian square. The genes segregate into those determining tall plants T and those determining dwarf plants, t. Then T and t re-combine as shown.

produced may be T or t . The zygote, of course, may have any combination from the two parents. How many combinations are possible? We have $T + T = TT$; $T + t = Tt$; $t + T = tT$; and $t + t = tt$. And that is *all!*

Another way of demonstrating this is by the use of the so-called *Mendelian square* shown here. This means that when two F_1 plants are mated, of any four offspring they have, one will have the genetic composition TT (or pure tall) ; one wiil have the genetic composition tt (or pure dwarf) ; and two will have the genetic composition Tt —or one gene for each in a mixed pair. These last two offspring will breed exactly like the F_1 generation.

This explanation, based upon Mendel's principle of segregation, shows us why his experiments gave the results they did. We can now re-do our original diagram:

Generation

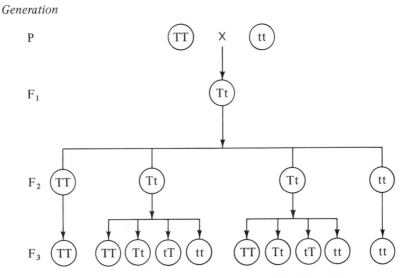

A diagram showing the probable genotypes resulting from the same cross illustrated in the drawing on page 104, but with letters chosen to indicate the dominant gene for tallness T and the recessive gene for dwarfness t.

Like any good scientist, Gregor Mendel proceeded to test his hypothesis with other experiments. Using pea varieties that produced round and wrinkled seeds, he demonstrated that roundness was dominant and that his hypothesis was an accurate prediction of what would happen when the two varieties were crossbred. More and more support for the hypothesis came from the work of later investigators, working with other plants, and with animals as well.

PRINCIPLE OF INDEPENDENT ASSORTMENT

Mendel also performed other, more complicated, experiments. He sought to find out, for example, what would happen if one crossbred simultaneously for two or more characteristics, say, height, seed shape, seed color, plant color, and so on. Each trait, he found, obeyed his principle of segregation, but there was no apparent connection between the inheritance of one trait and any other. Thus, if he crossed a plant that was of pure strain (with two identical genes) for both tallness (TT) and yellow color (YY) with a dwarf (tt) green (which is a recessive) (yy) plant, all the offspring would be, of course, tall and yellow, and would all have the gene combinations (Tt) and (Yy).

When these F_1 plants were mated, however, any combination of the parental genes was possible, from (TTyy) to (ttYY) to (TtYY) and so on. If you want to find out exactly what combinations are possible, and how many tall yellow, tall green, dwarf yellow, and dwarf green plants will be born in the F_2 generation, make up your own Mendelian square but with four boxes across, and four boxes down!

These experiments led Mendel to the statement of a second principle of genetics, the *principle of independent assortment:* the genes for each trait are separate from the genes for other traits and the inheritance of a gene for one trait has nothing to do with the inheritance of a gene for another trait. Any combination of genes for height and color, we have seen, is possible for the pea-plant. A plant of the F_2 generation with the genes (ttYY) (pure dwarf and pure yellow), for example, may be descended from a plant in the P generation that is pure tall and pure yellow (TTYY) —one trait has nothing to do with the other.

When Mendel's work was rediscovered in 1900, and its importance finally realized, geneticists (jen–et′–i–sists—students of genetics) began to make many more discoveries. One conclusion they came to, as a result of Mendel's work, was that *appearance* was not a dependable indication of genetic structure. This was a result of Mendel's demonstration of dominant and recessive characteristics. We have seen, for example, that a tall pea, in Mendel's P generation, when mated with a dwarf pea, would have offspring in the F_1 generation that would be fully as tall as the tall parent. In appearance, they would be the same, but their genetic make-up would be very different; the P plant would have the gene pair (TT) and could produce only tall offspring, while the "F₁-plant" would have the gene pair (Tt) and could have a dwarf offspring. Two new words had to be invented to express this difference: *genotype* (jeen′–o–type) for the genetic make-up of any organism, and *phenotype* (feen′–o–type) for the physical appearance of any organism, that is, the way it looks.

You are probably tired of all the new terms we have introduced in this chapter—gamete, zygote, independent assortment—and perhaps you wonder why it is necessary to introduce still new ones. But be patient. (As Lord Macaulay once put it, "Knowledge increases by steps, and not by leaps.") We shall shortly use these new terms, genotype and phenotype, to point out some very important implications of Mendel's discoveries—important for all biology, but particularly important for our study of human differences.

9

Genetics and Race

Following Mendel, we can say that his peas, in the F_1 generation, had the same *phenotype* as their tall parent, but had a *genotype* (Tt) that was different from *both* parents. Furthermore, when two F_1 plants were mated, they produced offspring with only two different phenotypes (three were tall, and one was dwarf), but with *three* different genotypes (one (TT), one (tt), and two (Tt))!

Further, if we look at the plants of the F_2 generation, and note there are three tall and one dwarf, we can even *predict* the genotype of the dwarf plant: it *must* be (tt), for if it had one (T) gene, it too would be tall. On the other hand, of the three tall F_2 plants, we can know only their phenotypes (tall) for we cannot detect which of the three has the genotype (TT) . Thus, when we know which trait is recessive (in this case, dwarfishness) , we know with certainty that the phenotype is the same as the genotype. With dominant traits, on the other hand, we cannot tell whether the phenotype represents a pure or a mixed genotype—we can only tell by the offspring they produce. A (TT) tall pea, for example, can never have dwarf offspring, while (Tt) tall peas can have them.

What has this to do with the races of mankind? Racial categories are normally set up on the basis of phenotype, not genotype!

Armed now with a knowledge of Mendel's work on the nature of inheritance, we can begin to see clearly the weaknesses in this type of classification. Let us use as an example the work of Madison Grant.

Grant claimed, you will remember, that the traits of the Nordic Great Race—blond, blue-eyed and superior—were recessive; therefore intermarriage with members of inferior races would cause permanent damage to the traits of the superior parent. From then on, he argued, the descendants of such a mixed marriage would resemble the inferior parent. All that could be said of such a statement, in the earlier chapter, was that it was incorrect. Now we can see *why* it is incorrect.

Weaknesses in Racial Arguments

Madison Grant, it is obvious, knew something of the work of Mendel and other geneticists, but he didn't understand it very well. Among humans, blue eyes are recessive and brown eyes are dominant. (Hair color and skin color are much more complicated, however, for reasons we shall give later.) Marriages between blue-eyed and brown-eyed people, therefore, result in offspring that are predictable according to Mendel's principles. If a person with genotype (BB) (two genes for brown eyes, which are dominant) marries a person with the genotype (bb) (two genes for blue eyes, which are recessive), then all their children will have brown eyes.

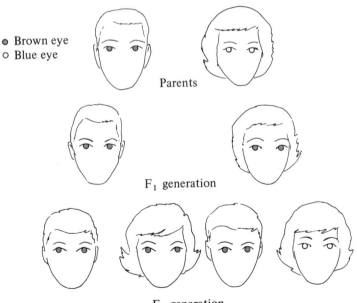

● Brown eye
○ Blue eye

Parents

F_1 generation

F_2 generation

The blue-eyed child in the F_2 generation is just as blue-eyed as is his blue-eyed ancestor in any previous generation.

Doesn't that sound, then, as if Madison Grant was right—that brown eyes have drowned out or have somehow overpowered blue eyes, and that all the descendants of the couple will resemble their brown-eyed ancestor? Well, it may sound that way to some. But we know better. First of all, while all the children in the F_1 generation have brown eyes—and resemble their brown-eyed parent in pheno-type—they have a genotype (Bb) which is different from those of *both* their parents. Secondly, if they were to marry people with genotypes like their own, in the next generation (F_2) one-fourth of the chil-dren would be blue-eyed again! And when such a blue-eyed child is born of brown-eyed parents, whether in the F_2 generation or in the F_{10} generation, that blue-eyed child is as thoroughly and completely blue-eyed—genotypically *and* phenotypically—as was his blue-eyed ancestor many generations ago! Remember Mendel's Principle of segregation: genes do not mingle or merge, but retain their identity as they are passed along from generation to generation.

Grant's other contention—that the Great Race was not only blue-eyed, but blond-haired, more intelligent, and so on, and that all these traits would disappear from descendants of a mixed marriage—is in violation of Mendel's second principle, the principle of independent assortment. We have seen, in the case of Mendel's peas, that a tall yellow plant could have tall green descendants, or dwarf yellow, or whatever. Genes for one trait are inherited *independently* of genes for other traits. Thus, if hair color and intelligence were each pro-duced by a single gene pair, as is eye color, and if a blonde, blue-eyed, intelligent person married a brown-haired, brown-eyed, un-intelligent person, just imagine how many varieties of descendants they could have! With a big enough Mendelian square, you could work out the combinations.

From a genetic point of view, there are at least two other weak-nesses to this idea of the superiority of the Great Race.

First of all, Madison Grant and other racists seem to consider certain traits superior to others. Anyone, of course, has the right to *prefer* blue eyes to brown eyes—or short noses to long ones, or red hair to black hair, or whatever. But preference is a matter of personal taste; it has nothing to do with *genetic* superiority or inferiority.

Can we, in fact, speak of a trait as being genetically superior or inferior? Only with difficulty. What we mean, at best, is that one trait is more *desirable* for one reason or another. It may be desirable because of the customs of one's society; some people think tall girls are more attractive, others think that short girls are more attractive.

Customs and taste, of course, vary from human group to human group: in Scandinavia where blond hair is very common, dark hair is considered very attractive by many people. In Italy, on the other hand, where dark hair is very common, blonde hair is often particularly admired. In some societies, especially where food shortages are common, fat women are considered highly attractive. In the United States, on the other hand, a slim figure seems to be more desirable, as witness most popular models and movie and television stars.

Most people who raise cattle would probably agree that short horns are to be preferred on the cattle to long horns—but if the cattle were able to vote, they might prefer long horns! Certain kinds of inherited diseases, or physical weaknesses, might certainly be considered genetic undesirables, but for the most part these seem to be associated with individuals, not with races. Since such weaknesses are frequently recessives we cannot accept Madison Grant's implication that recessive traits are superior to dominant ones. Nor is the reverse true, either, that recessives are *inferior* to dominants—there just doesn't seem to be any association, one way or another.

PURE VS. MIXED RACES

The second weakness, in genetic terms, in Madison Grant's argument has to do with his belief—shared by so many others—that some races are pure and some are mixed. Following Mendel, we now know that if a person has blue eyes (and we know that blue eyes is a recessive trait), then his genotype for eye color *must* be (bb) : both genes governing eye color are directives for blue-eyes. Geneticists would say that he is *homozygotic* (ho–mo–zy–got′–ic) for blue eyes. The word comes from the Greek word *homos,* meaning "same." In other words, the original zygote from which he developed had received identical genes for that trait from both parents.

On the other hand, a person with brown eyes (phenotype) may be either homozygotic for brown eyes (identical genes for brown eyes from each parent: (BB)), or he may be *heterozygotic* (*hetero-* from the Greek for "different") for eye color—having received a different gene from each parent ((Bb)).

The concept of pure and mixed races, then, is seen to raise many problems once we view the matter in genetic terms. Do we mean to imply that a member of a pure race is someone—and *only* someone— who is homozygotic for all traits? There is no such person, since there is genetic variation for some traits among all humans. (If not, all members of the population would look exactly alike.) Do we mean, then, that the member of the pure race is at least homozygotic for the traits we consider racially important, such as eye color? All right, then all blue-eyed people are members of one race, and all brown-eyed people are members of another race, correct? No. We are in difficulty, because some brown-eyed people are homozygotic and some are heterozygotic—and we can't tell which, at least until they have children. In other words, all blue-eyed people are pure (more accurately, homozygotic for that trait) and some brown-eyed people are also pure; but some brown-eyed people (the heterozygotic ones) are mixed. To which race shall we assign the last group? After all, they can have descendants who will be pure blue-eyed, pure brown-eyed, or mixed brown-eyed like themselves! If brown-eyed parents should have a blue-eyed child, does that mean that child and parents belong to different races?

If, in addition, we note—following Mendel's principle of independent assortment—that a person who is homozygotic for blue eyes could still very well be heterozygotic for hair color, skin color, head shape or whatever other traits are suggested, then it becomes apparent that Mendel's discoveries put an end to the old approaches to racial classification. At least, it did for those who make an effort to understand the implications of Mendel's work.

Nor is it a matter, solely, of his discoveries. Since 1900, geneticists have come to understand the nature of genetic inheritance in much more detail than Mendel could have imagined, though the credit for founding the science must of course be his.

Mendel, for example, was able to demonstrate that there were separate units of inheritance, that every individual must have a pair of each such units because he must inherit one of each pair from each of his parents, and so the sex cell—or gamete—must contain only one of each pair. As tremendous an advance as this knowledge was, it was still as far as Gregor Mendel could go. He did not know what these units—or genes—looked like, where they were located in the cells, and how they came together or separated.

CHROMOSOMES MAKE THE MAN

Later scientists were able to demonstrate that genes were in fact located on certain tiny string-like objects located in the center (nucleus) of every cell. These string-like objects were named *chromosomes* (kro'–mo–somes) and could just be seen, under a powerful microscope, under certain conditions. Chromosomes, it was found, varied slightly in shape; some curled like the letter S, some were

V-shaped and so on. Whatever the shapes, they normally came in pairs: two S-shaped chromosomes, two V-shaped chromosomes, etc.

It was decided, therefore, that a chromosome was a string of genes, that one of the pair was inherited from the father and one from the mother, and that each species of plant or animal had a characteristic number of chromosomes. Human beings, for example, normally have forty-six chromosomes, arranged in twenty-three pairs, in their cells. A sex cell, of course, has only twenty-three chromosomes, one from each pair, and will fuse with the set from the other parent in the new zygote to form a new set of forty-six.

Cells, in all living things, die and are replaced. If you have ever skinned your knee you have seen how new skin grows, slowly, to cover the wound. New skin cells, in such a case, are being produced, and—like all cells—are produced by the division of one old cell into two new, identical ones.

For all cells except the sex cells this division takes place in much the same way. It is at the moment when the cell is ready to begin the process of division called *mitosis* (my–toe′–sis) that, looking through a microscope, you can see the chromosomes in the nucleus. Each member of the pair divides in two, the long way, so that now the cell has *four* of each kind (see drawing) . As the cell begins to split in two (see Step 3) , one pair of each type of chromosome moves in each direction. When the division is completed (Step 4) the nucleus of each daughter cell has the same pairs, and the same number, of

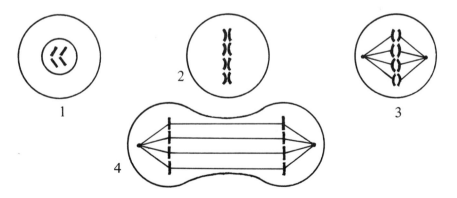

Mitosis: (1) A cell in its normal state. (2) The chromosomes divide lengthwise exactly in half. (3) The chromosomes move to opposite ends of the cell and (4) the cell starts to divide. Two new cells form, each containing exactly the same number of chromosomes as the original cell.

chromosomes as did the parent cell. After division is complete, the chromosomes appear to merge together, until it is time for the next division, when they separate and become distinct again.

In the case of sex cells (those that produce gametes), a different kind of division takes place, called *meiosis* (my–o'–sis). When the cell divides, no splitting of chromosomes takes place, so the daughter cells receive only one of each pair. This is necessary to prevent a doubling of the number of chromosomes in each generation.

Still more discoveries were made over the years, until, in 1952, two young biochemists—F. H. C. Crick, an Englishman, and James D. Watson, an American—were able to demonstrate exactly how a chromosome was constructed, and how—during division—it was able to duplicate itself.

Briefly, Crick and Watson showed that a chromosome was a giant molecule, made up in turn of many tiny molecules arranged in two strings. The two strings wind around each other like a pair of inter-twined snakes. If you want some idea of how this might look, take two short pieces of string, hold them together, and then twist them around each other until they form a new string of two twisted strands. For our purposes it is better, however, to think of a ladder, the sides of which are twisted around each other. Thus the two strings we talked about would be the sides of the ladder. These are

DNA. The two twisted chains are made of alternating sugar and phosphate molecules linked end to end. Cross-linking is not shown. S stands for a sugar molecule, P for a phosphate molecule.

formed of alternating pairs of sugar and phosphate molecules, as shown, and needn't detain us here. It is the *rungs* of the ladder that are most interesting to us. For it is here that the chromosome performs its trick of duplicating itself.

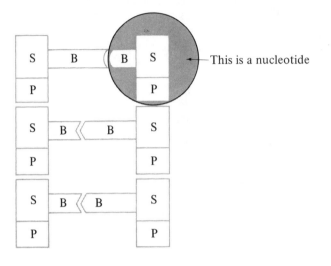

S = Sugar molecule   B = Base

P = Phosphate group

DNA, showing how the two strands are cross-linked through nucleotide bases. B stands for base.

Each rung consists of *two* parts, called bases, with each base connected to one of the sugar/phosphate pairs along the ladder. Together a sugar/phosphate/base molecule constitutes a *nucleotide,* as shown in the drawing.

For the sake of simplicity we shall now ignore the sides of the ladder, the sugars and phosphates, since these only repeat themselves, and think of the ladder as strings composed only of bases. It turns out that, for our purposes, there are four types of bases. These are adenine, cytosine, guanine and thymine. Let us call them, for short, A, C, G and T. Each string in the chromosome, then, can be thought of as an arrangement of many of these bases, in any possible order, say, AAACAGGTACTTG, or GCTAGGTATACCC, or whatever. As we have seen, the second string is constructed like the first, and the two strands wind around each other. (Actually, the sides of our twisted ladder, which is sometimes also referred to as a spiral staircase, is more correctly a *helix* and so the giant molecule is in the form of a double helix.

Each of the small bases in one strand is bound, or chemically attached, to the base on the other strand. There is one curious thing about this connection, however: an A molecule on one strand can only be bound to a T molecule on the other strand, while a C molecule can only be bound to a G. This is true for all life forms, and means that if you know the composition of one strand, you know the composition of the opposite strand. If one strand is made up of the string of bases AGGATCTC, *etc.,* then the opposing strand begins TCCTAGAG, *etc.* Normally, Crick and Watson argued, the two strands are, in a sense, attached to each other, for each molecule on one strand is chemically bound to its opposite number on the other

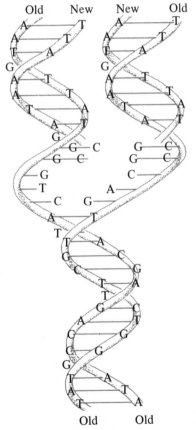

How nuclei split and make duplicates of themselves.

strand. The two strands (including the sugars and phosphates), twisting in helical fashion around each other, form one chromosome.

During mitosis, you may remember, each pair of chromosomes in a cell turns into four chromosomes. The work done by Crick and Watson enables us to understand how. During mitosis, they argued, the chemical bond disappears between the bases of the two strands making up a chromosome. As the strands separate (just as you might pull apart the two pieces of string you had twisted together), each molecule, on each strand, seems to draw upon the surrounding chemical substances and cause a *new* molecule to attach itself in the proper place. Naturally, an A molecule on the strand draws a T molecule to itself; a T draws an A; a G draws a C; and a C draws a G. Therefore, when the two old strands have completely separated, each strand has not only produced a new one to attach to itself, but it has duplicated exactly the one to which it was attached before! This is called the process of *replication,* and it happens in exactly the same way among *all* living things, from microscopic one-celled creatures to mammals and man himself. Here, in basic chemical terms, is the reason you resemble at least one of your parents.

Not only is the process of replication the same for all living things—plant or animal, insect or bird, amoeba or man—but the strands making up the chromosome are made up of combinations of the same four—and only these four—basic molecules! And, furthermore, what we have been calling a gene—a directive for some trait in the adult organism—is really just a sequence of small molecules (bases) on the strands. Each double helix is, as we noted, a giant molecule itself, and has an uncomfortably long name: deoxyribonucleic acid. We call it DNA for short.

In other words, a fairly long sequence of nucleotides on one DNA strand makes up a gene and can, when paired with another sequence or gene, determine some trait in an organism. The trait might be the shape of the red blood cell, or it might be the number of fingers on each hand—or it might be hair color, or whatever.

Why, then, do you look so different from a geranium or a giraffe? Only because, first, the number of pairs of chromosomes in the nucleus of one of your cells is different from the number in a geranium or giraffe cell, and second, because the arrangement of A,T,C,G molecules on *your* chromosomes follows patterns that are characteristic of human DNA, while the arrangements on giraffe and geranium chromosomes follow patterns characteristic of their species.

In fact, the DNA arrangements in a given species is almost identical for all members of the species; perhaps *ninety-five percent* of the sequences of A,T,C,G molecules are identical for *all* human beings. (It would *have* to be, otherwise a person would not be recognizable as human!) The differences in the remaining five percent are responsible for all the differences in appearance between individuals or groups.

The last two chapters have been difficult but necessary. Not only have we learned why Madison Grant's arguments were constructed on false notions, but we have begun to see why this is equally true of many ideas of racial differences.

To put it briefly, racial categories are generally based on phenotype, not genotype, and so are not really valid genetic classifications.

Equally important, however, we are now in a position to understand the source of the changes that produce new traits, and ultimately, new species and even new forms of life. We can begin to come to grips with the question of whether varieties of mankind are on their way to becoming new and separate species. We shall address ourselves to those problems in the next chapter.

10

Random Change and Selective Advantage

It may have occurred to you that the two kinds of trait we have discussed, namely dominant and recessive, may not cover all the possibilities. Sometimes, for example, it happens that neither trait is dominant. In other cases, more than one pair of genes is involved in a particular trait. In the matter of human skin color, for example, *six pairs* of genes direct the appearance of the trait. In such cases, and hair color would be another example, the heterozygotic offspring is not simply like one parent or the other, but exhibits a mixture, or blend, of both traits. All genes, however, as we know from Mendel's work, remain segregated.

There is another question, of very great importance, that may have occurred to you. Where do *new* traits come from? Aren't children born, sometimes—to animals and plants—who in some way small or large resemble neither of their parents and none of their ancestors? The answer is that of course this happens—but until now we have been discussing the *normal,* or *usual* pattern of genetic inheritance. But there certainly are exceptions to the ordinary pattern, and these exceptions are not only interesting but are responsible for *all* the variations and differences in life forms to be seen on earth! It would not be going too far, in fact, to say that if mistakes in genetic inheritance did not take place occasionally in all life forms, life would long since have died out on our planet. For it is these small changes that have enabled living things to cope with changes in the environment that might otherwise have wiped them out.

But—if a parent passes one of his set of genes on to his offspring, as Mendel pointed out, and if the offspring acquires pairs of genes (on matching chromosomes) from his parents, and if the genes direct what the adult trait will be, how can variation occur?

How Mistakes Occur

We have learned that the chromosome is composed of two twisting strands. Each of these strands is a giant molecule, called DNA, made up of a chain of smaller molecules for which we have used the letters A, T, C, and G. These smaller molecules are in turn made up of atoms of certain basic elements fixed together. Carbon, nitrogen, hydrogen and oxygen are the basic elements. One combination of atoms of these four elements form a molecule we call *adenine;* a slightly different combination forms a molecule we call *guanine.* These are illustrated in the drawing.

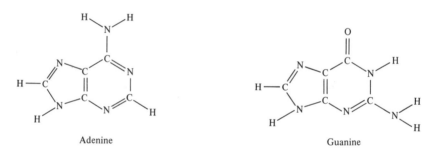

Adenine   Guanine

Notice the close similarity of adenine and guanine in chemical structure.

Although these atoms are usually permanently attached to one another, it can happen—for various reasons—that sometimes an atom or group of atoms of one kind breaks away and a different one from the surrounding chemical substance or from another part of the molecule attaches itself in its place. For example, if you look carefully at the two drawings, you will see that they are very similar. It would take only a slight rearrangement of the outer atoms (outside the two closed rings, that is) plus one addition to convert the adenine to a guanine. If this were to happen to the first base in a DNA chain ATTGGC, etc., the chain would then be GTTGGC, etc.

Of course, as we have learned, molecules on one chain of a double helix can only be bound to certain other molecules on the other chain: A to T, but G to C, for example. Therefore, if the change mentioned above were to occur, when the cell divides and the DNA strands separate and replicate, the new DNA strand GTTGGC, etc. will cause a new strand to develop beginning CAACCG, etc. From then on, replication will continue with the new arrangement of molecules, until some new change occurs.

Other forms of change can occur during the division of a cell. A long DNA strand can break, so that what was one long chromosome becomes from then on two smaller chromosomes—which continue to reproduce themselves separately from then on. Sometimes, two small strands become attached, forming a new long chromosome. It can happen in the process of replication that a DNA strand breaks into two parts and then rejoins, but one of the parts turns upside down before rejoining. Whatever the accident or change, the new DNA continues to reproduce itself from then on in its new form.

MUTATIONS

Such accidents, or changes in genetic structure, are called *mutations* (myoo–tay'–shuns) and are relatively rare. For the most part DNA molecules replicate themselves exactly and without trouble. When you reflect that there are billions of cells in any animal body, and that these cells are continually dividing and producing new cells, even rare events can add up to a fairly large number. But no matter how large the number, when they occur in the ordinary cells of the body, they will have no effect on the next generation.

What does matter to the next generation is a mutation in a sex cell when the cell is in the process of meiosis (dividing to form gametes). If a gamete contains a mutation in its genetic structure, then one or more genes have been changed, and this means that the offspring produced by that gamete will, in one trait or another, *not resemble* its parent, though it may pass its new genetic structure on to its descendants.

Most mutations are believed to be *lethal*. That is, a mutation may have so changed the genetic structure that the gamete is unable to join with the game from the other parent to form a zygote. After all, the chromosomes from one parent must be able to match with chromosomes from the other parent. Even if a zygote is formed, the genetic directives may be so confused that it cannot grow into a living organism, and dies before it is born. Or if it is born, the organism may die soon after birth. In many cases of mutation where the organism does survive and grow, it turns out to be sterile; it cannot have any offspring of its own.

While mutations are rare, those which permit the organism to survive and pass the mutation on to its descendants are rarer still. In such cases, the mutation is usually a very minor one, often hardly detectable. A child may have a little more body hair than either of its parents, or a little less. A maple tree may have leaves of slightly different shape than any of its ancestors; a dog may be born with a slightly longer tail. The mutation may be internal—a change in the shape of the liver. Or it may be in the body chemistry, say, in the secretion from some gland. Many living organisms, animal or plant, have in their genetic structure such minor mutations. Where they are noticeable at all, they account for some of the slight differences in appearance between parent and offspring. Other differences may be due to heterozygosity, or to differences in diet or other experiences of the offspring.

Mutations are random and rare. They are hardly ever passed on to future generations. Nevertheless, some mutations do get passed on. About once in every two million human births, for example, a baby is born with a mutation which produces *hemophilia*—the blood of the baby lacks the ability to clot when it is exposed to air. This makes any kind of cut on the skin very dangerous, since the child can bleed to death from even a small wound. If the child does survive and reproduce however, he may pass this very unwelcome trait on to his descendants.

It certainly sounds as if mutations are very undesirable things to have. Nevertheless, all the differences between all life forms have come about through mutations; that is why animals are different from plants, why land animals are so different from the sea animals from whom they are descended, and why we look different (and act differently) from our closest relatives the gorillas and chimpanzees.

Some mutations, then, are *desirable* or *favorable* and others are not; but how can we distinguish between them? And if a useful mutation should appear, how does it spread to the rest of the population? The elephant's trunk, the giraffe's long neck, the seal's flippers, the horse's hoof, and man's brain are all the result of successful mutations. But how did they spread, and why didn't the horse develop a trunk or the elephant flippers?

For the answers to such questions we must return to Charles Darwin and his theory of natural selection—although we now know much more about how that process occurs than he did.

BIOLOGICAL ISOLATE

Almost all living things require the presence of others of their kind for survival, and even more, for reproduction. Observe the stately oak, majestic and solitary in a forest of pine trees. It may be alone now, but once in the past there must have been two oaks within mating distance of each other—its parents. And if there are no other oaks somewhere nearby then our stately oak will have no descendants. No, the oak may seem alone to us, like the one mouse in your cellar or the eagle soaring overhead, but each is really a member of a biological community of its own kind.

We call such a community of living things a *biological* (or *breeding*) *isolate;* this is the largest group within which an organism is likely to choose a mate. Imagine an island in the ocean. There are mice on the island, snakes that eat mice, and birds that eat both snakes and mice. There are crabs along the shore and flowers and trees in the interior. Each of these life forms belongs to its own community. Snakes do not mate with flowers, nor crabs with mice, and so the individual must find its mate among the population of its own kind on the island. If there are ten thousand mice present, then together they form the isolate of the mice; if there are only a thousand garter snakes, then that is their isolate.

If you think about it, the expression biological isolate is not entirely correct, because an isolate is rarely completely isolated. Even on our island, while most individuals will choose their mates from their respective isolates, a few may not. Perhaps a mouse or a snake may float on a piece of driftwood to the next island and find a mate there. A crab may swim or a bird may fly to another place, and the wind may blow the seeds of trees and flowers far away. Most of those who read this book will marry someone of their own country, but a few will find husbands and wives on far distant continents.

A biological isolate, therefore, is not necessarily completely closed off—but it is largely closed off; most of its members will find their mates within it, a few will find mates in other biological isolates of the same species.

Perhaps, in fact, we should think of a species as the largest possible biological isolate; it is the combination of all the smaller isolates, and is the largest possible group in which an individual can find a mate. For, if you will remember, we said in a previous chapter that a species is the largest group of a particular life form in which reproduction is possible, or at least in which viable offspring can be produced. On our island, there are both mice and snakes, but they belong to separate species and cannot mate. On the other hand, a mouse of our island can—if he reaches the mainland—mate with a mouse he finds there.

Earlier, we simply gave this as a definition of species. Now, of course, you have some understanding of why a mouse and snake cannot mate. Each may produce a sex gamete, but the gametes cannot join and form a zygote. Each gamete has a different number of chromosomes, and the DNA in each chromosome is so different that matching is not possible. Even when two species are closely related within the same genus, as in the case of horse and donkey, viable offspring cannot be produced. Enough chromosomes are similar, in such a case, for the zygote to be formed and for a living offspring (in this case a mule) to be born. The DNA and chromosomes are so different, however, that meiosis is not possible. Hence the mule cannot produce gametes and so cannot have offspring of his own.

FORMATION OF NEW SPECIES

All of this is very important for an understanding of how mutation contributes to the formation of new species. Let us return to our island. There were, we pretended, some ten thousand mice on the island, forming a biological isolate. To the casual eye, these mice all look alike. If we examine them closely, however, we are likely to find slight differences among them. They may all be grey of fur, but some may be a slightly darker grey, some lighter, some almost a brownish-grey. Some are very furry, some have less heavy coats. There are differences in size, in speed, in ability to digest different foods, and so on.

Suppose we could examine the genetic structure of the mice in this island population, and we found that there were different genes present on the island for fur color, tail size, and so on. Let us pretend that we can identify each gene and describe each genotype.

Eighty percent of the mice have a gene producing a long tail. The other twenty percent have a gene for a short tail. The term for the percentage of occurrence of a gene is *genetic frequency*. We would say that the genetic frequency of the first gene is 80 percent and of the second 20 percent. (In a similar way, you could count the number of people in your class with blue eyes and determine the frequency, in your class, of homozygosity for blue eyes. But of course you couldn't determine the frequency of the *gene* for blue eyes until you knew how many of your classmates with brown eyes were homozygotic and how many were heterozygotic.

Returning to the mice of our island, we note again that long tails are in the majority, with a genetic frequency of 80 percent. Perhaps on the mainland the frequency is reversed, and long tails have a frequency of only 20 percent. Does that mean that a short-tailed mouse on our island is really a stranger? After all, he is a member of a minority. Shouldn't he be counted as a member of the mainland mouse population, where short tails are in a majority? No, that is obviously silly. The short-tailed mouse is a member of the island's *mouse biological isolate,* even though the genetic frequency of his tail form is lower than for another tail form.

Let us take a look at the eyes of our mice. Suppose they are all brown. The genetic frequency for mouse eyes, then, on our island is brown, 100 percent. For this trait, there is no genetic variation. In fact let us suppose, even on the mainland, that there is no genetic variation, and all mice have brown eyes. The genetic frequency of blue eyes, among mice, is *zero.*

In this way, we could determine, for the population of any given biological isolate, what the genetic frequency was for any particular trait, from zero to one hundred percent. In theory, we might be able, eventually, to determine the frequency of *every* gene present in the mouse population. (Of course, we are still a long way from actually being able to do such a thing.) If we could, we would then be able to chart the type and frequency of every gene in the total *gene pool* of this biological isolate. By gene pool, we mean all the genes available to the descendants of the members of this mouse population. We know, for example, that a baby mouse born on this island may have a long or short tail, since genes for both traits are available in the gene pool of the isolate. Furthermore, we can predict that the baby mouse, born on the island, is much more likely to have a long tail than a baby mouse born on the mainland (because of the different frequencies of the genes in the two places). On the other hand, no baby mouse—in the normal course of events—is likely to be born on the island with blue eyes, since no gene for blue eyes is available in the gene pool. Finally, in each generation the frequency for each gene in the pool normally remains pretty much constant. If, in the P generation, we found the frequency for long tails to be 80 percent and for short tails 20 percent, we should find approximately the same frequency in the F_5 or the F_{15} generations.

The use of the word *normally* should alert us to the fact, as we have already seen, that there are exceptions. To begin with, suppose a baby mouse is born one day with blue eyes. This means, of course, that a mutation has taken place in the infant's genetic structure, but still it is a minor mutation, and we can expect the mouse to survive, grow up, mate, and have offspring. If blue eyes are a recessive, as they are among humans, they won't begin to show up again for two generations at least,* but after that we can expect to find blue-eyed mice. We would have to note that the frequency for brown eyes among our island mice is no longer 100 percent, but something less, and for blue eyes the frequency is no longer zero, but something more.

We noted, just a little way back, that *normally* the genetic frequency remains constant from generation to generation. Suppose, however, that this new trait—blue eyes—gave some sort of advantage to the mice born with it. It is difficult to imagine what that could be, since among humans blue-eyed and brown-eyed people seem to see equally well. Still, we have been pretending, so let us continue to do so, and pretend that mice born with blue eyes can detect snakes just a little bit better or faster than mice with brown eyes. If this were actually so, it would mean that blue-eyed mice had a slightly better chance of avoiding snakes, and thus staying alive and of having more children. Each generation, in that case, would have a slightly higher genetic frequency for blue eyes, and eventually—after enough time had passed—the whole mouse population of the island would have blue eyes.

If such a thing were actually to happen, we would say that blue eyes in mice was a favorable mutation, because it provided a *selective advantage*. Those mice who had it were better able to survive and have more offspring than those without it. By natural selection, therefore, the new trait spread through the population.

Usually, however, even the most favorable trait confers a disadvantage in some other respect. To continue with our game of pretend, we might imagine that, while blue eyes are better able to detect

---

* That is, a few of the offspring of the blue-eyed mouse, though brown-eyed, will each be carrying a recessive gene for blue eyes. If two of these happen to mate, at least one more blue-eyed mouse can be produced.

snakes lurking in the grass, perhaps brown eyes are better for finding seeds and other food. In such a case, the advantages of the two eye colors may well change from generation to generation. In one generation, food may be plentiful and so may snakes. In that case, blue-eyed mice will have the advantage. In the next generation, food and snakes may both be scarce, and brown-eyed mice will do better, and have more offspring. In still another generation, food may be plentiful and snakes scarce, and so eye color will not be much of a factor in determining which mice live and have offspring. If you were to study them during such a time, you would not be able to perceive any selective advantage for either eye color. This is a surprisingly important point, as we shall see later.

In any case, we have seen that mutations can and do occur in the genetic structure of any individual of any species, plant or animal. Such mutations are random or chance events. If the mutation occurs in the individual's sex cells, it will affect the appearance of the individual's offspring, assuming the change is small enough not to kill the offspring before birth or right after it. If the individual with the mutation survives and has offspring, it will pass the genetic change along. But the genetic frequency will remain small. If the mutation confers some selective advantage, then it will spread, through natural selection, throughout the biological breeding isolate. But if, through a change in the environment, it then confers some selective *dis*advantage, then—through natural selection—it will decrease in frequency and perhaps even disappear.

Selective advantage and disadvantage can change from generation to generation; but if a trait continues over enough time to provide selective advantage, it will spread to all members of the isolate. Given enough time it will even spread to other isolates, and throughout the species.

Sometimes, however, a breeding isolate (or a number of isolates) remains separate from the rest of the species for a very long time, perhaps tens of thousands of years. During this time, many small changes occur and spread through each segment of the species, but are not shared with the other segment. Then, when two representatives of the separated segments do meet and try to mate, we find they have been separated too long. Like horse and donkey, or lion and tiger (good examples of just such a thing), though they mate they can no longer produce viable offspring; their respective genetic structures have become, over time, simply too different. From the original species, two new species have developed.

An interesting aspect of *speciation* (the division of one original species into two or more new ones) is that the sister species cannot share in mutational changes, however advantageous they may be. Suppose a mutation for horns was to develop among donkeys, and it was so advantageous that within a short period of time (in evolutionary terms) it spread to *all* donkeys. Still, it could never spread to their close relatives, the horses. Horses and donkeys cannot produce viable offspring, and so genetic interchange is not possible.

Mutation, then, goes on all the time, and natural selection goes on all the time. In any population—human, animal, or plant—there is a frequency for any genetic trait, from zero to one hundred. We have seen that increase or decrease in frequency relates to selective advantage, and this can vary from generation to generation. It can vary because of differences in enemies, in sources and quantity of food. It can vary because of changes in climate or temperature, or for an untold number of other reasons.

Furthermore, a trait may be present in a population today for which no selective advantage or disadvantage can be discovered. Some people would argue that we must be patient; someday we will discover the significance of the trait. Why do some people have straight hair and some curly? Many arguments have been offered, but no one really knows for sure. And some scholars argue that there *is* no difference, that hair shape is simply a *non-adaptive* trait; it provides neither advantage nor disadvantage, but is just a meaningless difference. Others would argue that what we consider non-adaptive today may once have been important.

Let us go back to our story about mouse eye-color on an imaginary island. If the mice were studied when food was plentiful and snakes were scarce, who could tell the advantages and disadvantages of blue eyes and brown eyes? In the same way, it is argued that perhaps once, in man's ancestry, different hair shapes provided different kinds of advantage and disadvantage—all of which have long since become unimportant. If that is indeed so, perhaps we shall never find out about it.

IMPORTANCE OF DIFFERENCES

There is another side to the matter, however. As we stated earlier, whether individual differences are advantageous or disadvantageous, it is most important that there *be* differences! It is easy now to see why. If, in our imaginary island mouse population, there are both brown and blue eyes, they have a built-in advantage over some neighboring island with only one eye color. If the availability of food changes, or the danger from snakes changes, mice with one eye color or the other will do better—but, either way, the entire mouse population benefits! The gene frequency changes, in response to new conditions, and so the mice (as a group!) adapt . . . and survive.

In the history of the world many species—in fact, most of those that have ever existed—have come up against conditions beyond their ability for new adaptation. Such species have become extinct; that is, they died out, leaving no descendants. Those species present in the world today, including our own, are the ones that were able to adapt to whatever changes they encountered. They adapted to new foods, found ways of avoiding new enemies, adjusted to new temperatures and different climates. Somehow they survived, while their sister species died out. In this process of survival, a very important factor has always been *variability:* a gene pool exhibiting many choices for the future generations.

This is as true of man as of any other species. Let us turn now to the story of man's evolution; let us see how he came to be what he is today, so that we may better understand the importance or unimportance of present-day differences and variations among men.

11

Man's Early Ancestors

In December, 1938, a fisherman brought up an odd-looking fish off the coast of South Africa. It was a fine catch, about five feet long and weighing over one hundred pounds. But he was troubled; it was like nothing he had ever seen before. Particularly strange were four paddle-like, finned "arms" on the bottom of the fish.

Fortunately the fisherman decided not to use the fish for food; and thanks to the efforts of a local museum keeper, it was well enough preserved for a leading fish expert, J. L. B. Smith, to take a look at it.

Smith was in a state of high excitement—not because he couldn't identify the fish, but because he could. And it was as if he had been confronted with a living dinosaur. For this fish, which had been alive only a few days earlier, had been seen up to that time only in fossil form. It was without doubt a coelacanth (seal–a–kanth), a type of fish that had supposedly been extinct for some seventy million years! Several other specimens in good condition have been caught since the first one was taken.

Even aside from the fact that coelacanths are "living fossils," scientists have been especially interested in getting a good look at the creatures, for they are members of a larger group called *lobe-finned fishes* (official name: crossopterygians). The lobe part refers to the paddle-like fins, which contain more muscle and bone than most fins.

A model of a coelacanth fish. This group of fish was once believed to have become extinct 75,000,000 years ago. *American Museum of Natural History.*

These lobes (plus other adaptations having to do with an ability to obtain oxygen directly from the air) made it possible for the early lobe-fins to exist in the face of changing conditions, while other species of fish died out. When their streams or lakes became foul or dried out, they were able to "walk" to find water elsewhere.

As you may have gathered, these lobes were the forerunners to our legs and arms, and to the legs of all amphibians and land animals on earth—past and present.

An interesting aspect of the coelacanths is that they are creatures which, because of pressures of the environment, found it possible or necessary to become "full-time" fish again, even though their ancestors had been "part-time" land creatures and started the parade out of the sea.

But the lobes have remained as reminders of the lobe-fin's flirtation with the land some seventy million years ago. Clearly the adaptation is a genetic one and has been passed on from generation to generation. Of course the adaptation started with one or more mutations.

So mutations produce changes in genetic structure, which can help or hinder an organism in its effort to live and have offspring of its own. Those changes which are helpful spread by natural selection through the species. All life forms must continually find better ways to avoid their enemies and acquire food. The advantage provided by any one mutation is usually small, for there are always many enemies, and many other life forms are competing for the same food supply. This usually minimizes whatever advantage is conferred.

It happens, sometimes, that a life form is very fortunate and finds itself in a wonderful new environment where enemies are few and food is plentiful. In such cases, variation seems to increase. It might thus appear that many more new mutations are occurring. Actually, mutations continue to occur at the same rate as before; but with more than enough food for all and few enemies, almost all individuals, whatever their genetic makeup, will survive, have offspring, and pass their traits on to their descendants. Swiftly (in evolutionary terms), from the original species there will develop a large and varied population, from which many new species will branch off. Each new species will represent a degree of specialization in the new environment—each will find and inhabit its own ecological niche, or slot. After a while, however, the population will increase to the point where there will no longer be more than enough food for all; competition will increase, enemies will develop (every living form serves as food for some others), and evolutionary change will seem to slow down. Again, mutations will continue at the same rate, but because each new species has achieved a pretty good adaptation to its particular niche, fewer genetic changes will be likely to be passed on to descendants.

When a life form goes through such a sequence of events—from entry into a new and favorable environment, to increasing population with increased variety, to new speciation and the occupation of many ecological niches—we call the whole process *adaptive radiation*. New species are radiated out from the old one, each adapting to a special niche in the new total environment.

One of the most important of such events in the history of life on earth occurred many hundreds of millions of years ago, when one or more species of fish developed the ability to survive, at least for periods of time, on dry land. These were the lobe-fins. They could breathe air, instead of—or as well as—water, and they could slither through mud and sand instead of flopping about helplessly as most fish do when out of water. A whole new environment was opened up for them. Quantities of plant and insect life became available, with no enemies or competition. A tremendous population increase took place, and from these early lobe-fins developed all the forms of animal life that have backbones and breathe air, including frogs, lizards, birds, mammals, and man himself.

Another such event—particularly important in man's history—took place some sixty to seventy-five million years ago, as the great dinosaurs and other reptiles were dying out. Mammals—warm-blooded creatures, capable of bearing live young and suckling them—had existed on earth for some time, but they had been small creatures and relatively few. As reptiles disappeared, mammals replaced them all over the world, moving into the newly opened ecological niches and slowly adapting to them.

PRIMATES

In this period, some of the tiny mammals took to trees and began to adapt to the special kind of life this required. Food in trees was plentiful, consisting of leaves, berries, seeds, insects, and bird's eggs, and there were few enemies who could bother them in their tree homes. Adaptive radiation took place, and many new varieties of mammals soon appeared, adapted to life in the trees. Among them were various forms of what naturalists call *primates,* an order of mammals which includes all forms of monkeys, apes and man. In those early days, of course, all the primate species were just small monkey-like creatures, but present-day monkeys, apes, and man are descended from them.

How did primates differ from other mammals? The requirements for successful life in the trees were different from those for *terrestrial* life, that is, life on the surface of the earth. There was selective advantage, therefore, for the development and spread of traits useful in *arboreal* (tree) life, and primates share such traits. You can clasp your hands behind your back, for example, and so can any monkey, but a donkey can't bring its legs around its back and neither can a lion. Skeletal changes took place among the primates, permitting greater and more flexible movement of the limbs. Land animals go about, for the most part, on four limbs, in a posture which is called *pronograde* (the posture you would be in when your hands and knees). In trees, however, an *orthograde* (upright) posture is often more useful, and most primates developed such a posture.

But the posture of an animal is not simply a matter of skeleton. Digestion is different for pronograde and orthograde creatures, and so is the circulation of blood, and so you can see that many changes were taking place among primates, causing them to differ from other mammals. Stereoscopic vision, the ability to see in depth and thus to

An adult dusky lemur, one of the primates. Its feet and posture suit its tree habitat. *New York Zoological Society.*

judge distance accurately, is particularly important for life in trees, where a mistake in judgment may send you crashing to the ground, and primates are among the animals particularly characterized by this trait. The sense of smell, on the other hand, is not as useful for life in the trees as it is on the ground, and tends be much less developed among primates than among other animals. Again, such different emphasis on certain senses was related to differences in skull structure and brain structure between primates and other animals.

One of the most interesting—and important—aspects of adaptation to arboreal life for all primates had to do with the ends of their limbs; their hands and feet. The earliest mammals of seventy-five million or one hundred million years ago had primitive, unspecialized fore-paws, not unlike those of many lizards today. That is, at the end of each limb were five finger-like digits, each ending in a claw-like nail. As mammals adapted to life on earth the ends of their limbs became more specialized, and thus more effective for life on the ground. Members of the cat and wolf families, for example, developed true paws, with protective pads, and very short digits with long, sharp claws. They could run swiftly on such paws, then use their claws to hold and tear their prey. All cats but the cheetah have retractable claws. Other creatures developed hoofs, the equivalent of our feet, making possible great swiftness to carry their owners away from danger. The horse, for example, runs nimbly on a single hoof on each leg that has evolved from the nail of their middle toes! The other toes, unneeded, have over time and through the evolutionary processes of mutation and natural selection, practically disappeared.

For primates, the original primitive lizard-like hands, with long flexible digits and short claws or nails, proved most useful for life in the trees. No specialization into paws or hoofs ever took place, there-fore, and the hands and feet of all primates remained relatively unchanged. You have probably noticed how similar to human hands are the feet of lizards; well, you had it turned around: human hands look like those of lizards because there has been little evolutionary change in these parts of our bodies! All primates, with the exception of man, have in fact *four* hands, one at the end of each limb. Man alone underwent a later evolutionary change, in which the two hands at the end of his legs developed into feet.

But that happened much later. In the period around sixty million years ago, man's ancestors were just one of the many species of small primates adapting to arboreal life. By about forty to fifty million years ago, specialization had taken place among the primates to the point where we can distinguish the ancestors of the three super-families of the primate order.

One group of primates living at that time would give rise to the monkeys of the New World, of North and South America: the spider monkeys, the marmosets, and their many relatives.

A second group of primates of that period was to develop into the Old World monkeys (of Africa, Europe and Asia) : the macaques, baboons, and many others.

MAN-LIKE PRIMATES

The third group of early primates gave rise to the superfamily known as *Hominoidea* (hom–in–oid'–ee–uh), which means "man-like." This superfamily has within it two families, one containing the gorilla, the chimpanzee, orang-utan, and the gibbon, plus their ancestors and extinct relations, and the other containing only man and his ancestors and extinct relatives. In the period to which we are referring—some fifty million years ago—it is only possible to say that a certain fossil primate is ancestral to hominoids in general; we cannot know whether its particular descendants became gorillas, men, both, or neither. Indeed, the question has no meaning, for the two lines had probably not yet separated.

If we think about it, it is rather impressive that scholars can determine as much as they can. After all, the primates of fifty million years ago were tiny creatures, few of them as large even as a modern squirrel, though the early hominoids were, on the whole, somewhat larger than most of the other primates of the time. All we find of them, when we are lucky enough to find anything, are a few weathered, tiny fragments of fossilized bone, usually of the jaw or skull, sometimes containing a tooth or two. How, then, can scholars be certain that one fragment represents an early primate who was to give rise to New World monkeys, while another tiny fragment represents an ancestor of an Old World monkey?

The answer is that, first, the scholars are rarely certain. Mistakes are often made, there are many disagreements, and the scholars often change their minds. However, there are some clues and hints to be found, even in tiny pieces of bone and tooth; and when a number of separate bits of evidence all point to the same conclusion, then the scholar may, with trepidation, use the term *certain*.

As we remember from our discussion of speciation, when two lines separate into different species it becomes impossible for them to share in the changes in one another's gene pool. Humans have feet, and we have noted that no other primate does. If, therefore, a scien-

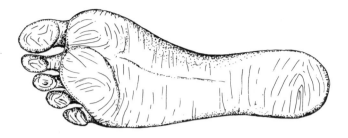

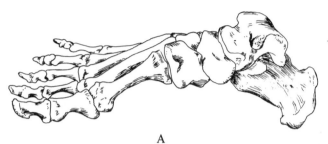

A

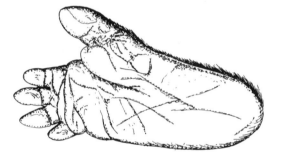

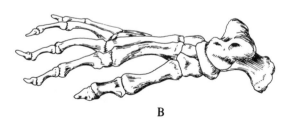

B

The human foot (A), compared to the foot of a gorilla (B). The gorilla has a prehensile toe. The skeletal side views reveal differing development of basically the same bone structure. Adapted from Buettner-Janush, *Origins of Man,* Wiley.

tist were to find a fossil fragment of some early primate's foot bone—
as distinguished from any *hand* bone—that would be enough of a clue
that the creature whose bone he held must be an ancestor of man or,
at least, a close relative of man. One thing is certain: the primate
couldn't have been an ancestor of any monkey or ape alive today, for
none of them shared in the genetic changes that produced the human
foot. The foot, of course, was far more useful than the lower "hand"
for life on the ground, and was an important factor in our ancestors'
success when they came down out of the trees, for the foot developed
soon after that event took place.

In the same way, there are tiny, but important, differences in
tooth, jaw, and skull shape, and so on, which indicate to the scientist
that a particular fossil primate of fifty million years ago was com-
mitted to the New World monkey line, or the Old World monkey
line, or the hominoid line. Very possibly, among the hominoid line
there was a species which would develop in the direction of man, but
if so we cannot detect it at so early a time. It is possible that the lines
of man and great apes had not yet separated, and were but varieties of
a single species.

By fifteen to twenty million years ago, there can be little doubt
that the hominoid lines had separated into two distinct subfamilies,
one that contained the ancestors of the great apes, and one that we
call *Hominidae* (ha–min'–i–day)—not man-*like* (hominoid) but
hominid, that is, ancestral to true men!

But both groups of that period were apparently a very successful
life form. They ranged over much of what is today Africa, Europe
and Asia, and there were certainly many varieties; scholars still
debate—and will continue to do so for a long time—over how many
species and genera of hominoids there actually may have been. One
name has come into use for most of the hominoids of the time—*Dryo-
pithecinae* (dry-o–pith–ah–see'–nay)—which comes from the Greek
words for tree-apes. In size they varied from that of a small present
monkey to larger ones almost as big as a modern chimpanzee. Many
dryopithecine species no doubt became extinct long ago. There are
some fossils that scholars believe were ancestral to modern gorillas,
chimpanzees, orang-utans, and gibbons—the great apes of today—although there is argument and uncertainty about which fossil is
ancestral to which great ape.

One fossil, however, has produced increasing interest among scientists. A few fossil fragments of a dryopithecine-like creature—bits of a

lower jaw and a few teeth—were found some years ago in India, in the foothills of the Himalaya mountain range. The creature—quite small, hardly as large as a modern gibbon—was named *Ramapithecus* (rama–pith'–eh–kus: Rama's ape) in honor of Lord Rama. In Indian religious literature, Lord Rama is said to have enlisted the aid of apes in his war against evil. From the name we can see that those who first studied it believed it to be just another ape of the dryopithecine type. Further study, however, has caused many to revise their opinion.

It is now believed, increasingly, that Ramapithecus was the dryopithecine type from which man is descended. The teeth and jaw shape are sufficiently different from those of all the other dryopithecines that most scholars are satisfied that *Ramapithecus* was developing in the direction of humans. *Ramapithecus* was apparently quite a sturdy little creature, for a number of fossils of this type have turned up, not only in India but as far away as East Africa. It is believed by many scholars that there was no more than one genus of ramapithecines, and some would even argue that all the fossils came from only one species! If that should turn out to be so, then man is descended from the *Ramapithecus* of fourteen or fifteen million years ago.

Ramapithecus is so interesting that we wish we knew much more about him. Was he, indeed, a tree-ape like the other dryopithecines, or had he made the transition from tree life to ground life that was so important in the history of man's development? Until we find some fossil fragments of his feet, or of some other parts of his skeleton, we cannot know for sure. His teeth were very much like human teeth, as we noted, and different from that of apes. What, then, did *Ramapithecus* eat? A difference in diet may have been very important, for the great apes today live mostly on fruit and insects, while man eats a great variety of foods, including meat.

We cannot yet answer these questions with any certainty, but we do know what must have happened to man's ancestors around the time of *Ramapithecus,* perhaps a little later or even a little earlier. Sometime around ten or fifteen million years ago, the tree-apes who were to give rise to man left the trees and became an unusual primate, one that began to adapt to life on the ground. The early period of this new life, it would certainly seem, must have been dangerous and difficult for the small, monkey-like creature. It had to escape from meat-eating enemies by running away, not by climbing higher; yet the hands at the end of its lower limbs were better adapted to climbing than to running. It had to find food on land; yet it was adapted better to finding food in trees.

Why, then, did this ancestral primate leave the security of arboreal (tree) life for the dangers and difficulties of life on the ground? We cannot *know* the reason, of course, but we can try to imagine. A very reasonable guess is that it had no choice; somewhere, sometime, perhaps because of changes in climate, what had been a forested area changed into a treeless grassland. Such changes can take hundreds, even thousands, of years, and usually the animals adapted to life in the trees retreat with the treeline, or die out. Our ancestors, however—perhaps the ramapithecines themselves—were unable to retreat for some reason, and just refused to die out. They scrabbled for roots and berries and small animals; they hid among rocks and caves; they managed to escape from the large hunting animals.

Under such conditions, there must have been great selective advantage for certain traits. Size and strength were very helpful in survival, and over time our ancestors began to grow larger and stronger. The hands on the lower limbs evolved into feet that were useless for grasping, but very useful for swiftly running after game and away from enemies. The lower limbs became legs, long and strong—again, for running. Many other changes took place in the body structure, permitting our ancestors to stand—and run—upright, and to acquire food. The primate brain is a good one but the early hominid on the ground required an even better one for survival. Eventually a brain evolved that was larger and capable of more complex thinking.

These are some of the things that must have taken place on the basis of what man was to look like later. The fossil information, unfortunately, is very skimpy. After *Ramapithecus,* we have no hominid fossils for the next ten million years—just the period when all these important changes were taking place. Why not? We simply do not know. Some people think that man's ancestors were very few, others suppose that as the early hominids grew more intelligent, they avoided falling into swamps and bogs, and so they left few fossils of the kind other animals left. More likely, there are fossils for this period somewhere in the world, but we have not yet found the proper geological beds. What excitement there will be in scientific circles when such fossils are found!

In any case, the curtain comes down on man's early history with *Ramapithecus,* some fourteen million years ago, and does not rise again until about two to three million years ago. From that point on, however, the fossil record is good, and is getting better all the time. We shall discuss these fossils in the next chapter.

12

Man Emerges

In 1925, a child playing near the town of Taung, in South Africa, found a strange looking skull. Eventually, it found its way to Raymond Dart, an anatomist and physical anthropologist, who cleaned it and studied it carefully. He named it *Australopithecus africanus* (aus–tral–o–pith–ee′–kus af–ri–kan′–us) which means the southern ape, African species. Although he named it an "ape," Dart became convinced in time that his "Taung's baby" (It was the skull of a small child) represented an early hominid, perhaps ancestral to man. More and more australopithecine (aus–tral–o–pith′–eh–seen) fossils began to turn up, and Dart and his associates studied them. Some scholars were convinced that these creatures were early humans, but others disagreed, and there was much argument in scientific circles.

In recent years, Louis L. B. Leakey and members of his family have made a number of exciting australopithecine finds in a canyon-like place known as Olduvai Gorge, in eastern Africa. Other australopithecines have been identified in Java, China, northern Africa, and southwestern Asia, but the largest number come from southern and eastern Africa.

There are still many points in dispute, such as the number of australopithecine genera and species, and which, if any, were directly ancestral to man himself. Most scholars now tend to agree on certain things about the australopithecines. We can say with some assurance that in the period from about two and a half million years ago to about three-quarters of a million years ago, the hominids on earth were represented by australopithecines. There may have been more than one species; there may even have been more than one genus. All we know for sure is that among them was the species from which man is descended.

The australopithecines varied in size, but they averaged under five feet in height. This makes them smaller, on the average, than most modern humans, except perhaps for Pygmies; but they were much larger and sturdier than the earlier ramapithecines. We have accumulated a considerable amount of australopithecine skeletal material, and there can be no doubt that they walked upright on two legs, with what we would recognize as feet at the end. In fact, from the neck down, an australopithecine would be difficult to tell from a modern, small human. By two million years ago, the human body, not counting the head, had evolved pretty much into its present form. Above the neck, however, we find a skull that strikes us as more ape-like than human. But if we study it closely, we find that the teeth are quite human, and the brain, though still small by human standards, is larger in comparison with the size of its owner than that of any ape brain we know of. *Australopithecus,* many scholars now believe, was definitely a hominid, and should be classified as a member of the genus *Homo* along with modern man. They argue that his classification should be changed to *Homo africanus,* with all the varieties of australopithecines simply subspecies—different types of the same species from different places and times. Others, including Professor Leakey, argue that there were at least *two* genera of *Australopithecus,* from only one of which we are descended, while the other line became extinct.

Tools and Weapons

Since we cannot, in this book, settle this argument, let us leave it and turn to what is probably the most exciting thing about the australopithecines, or, at least, some of them: *they could make tools and weapons!* By about one or two million years ago, someone on earth (and Australopithecus is obviously the best candidate) was able to chip stone in a crude but definitely recognizable way. The tools may have been used to crack bones or nuts to extract the food inside. They may have been used for digging roots, for defense, and perhaps even in hunting.

Have you ever tried to chip a rock with another rock? It isn't easy. It takes practice, and perhaps training. It is much easier to chip a block of wood with a sharp rock, or a piece of horn or bone; and so some scholars, such as Raymond Dart, have argued that if we are certain the australopithecines could work stone into tools we have to conclude that they could work with other, easier, materials, which simply have not survived to the present time.

Others go even further and point out that this ability to work stone in a recognizable way indicates that older ones must have taught the younger ones. How could they teach? Did they have the beginnings of language? We can only speculate, we do not know. Again, some of the South African australopithecine fossils have come from caves which contained many baboon bones. This has led some to speculate that the australopithecines were hunting baboons for food. But the baboon is a fierce animal, perhaps as dangerous as a leopard or a wolf. It is hard to imagine *one* small australopthecine, even armed with a chipped rock, hunting and killing baboons regularly for food. Did this mean that australopithecines were organized into bands, with leaders and discipline, so that a group of male australopithecines went out hunting regularly, trapping and clubbing baboons to death?

This is, of course, all speculation, but it does seem to many anthropologists that one million or more years ago, man's australopithecine ancestors had tools and weapons, and even the beginnings of human social organization, however ape-like his head may still have been.

By about a half a million years ago, man had changed so much in the direction of modern man from the earlier Homo africanus or australopithecine types, that a new classification is usually used. Unfortunately, the name that most use—*pithecanthropine* (pith–ee–can'–throw–peen) —comes from the Greek for ape-man and makes us imagine something much less human than he really was. The first remains of this early human were found so long ago, you see, that the scientists who studied it were unable to realize its true nature.

The story of how it was found, however, is one of the most exciting in the history of man's search for his ancestors. You will remember that Charles Darwin, toward the end of the nineteenth century, published his works on the theory of evolution. In them, he argued that man, like all other animals, had evolved into his present form from some earlier types, more ape-like in appearance. Those who rejected his ideas—particularly as they related to man—demanded to know what his evidence was for such a statement. If man had evolved from some earlier creature, they said, could Darwin or anyone show some examples of that earlier creature? You must understand that, at this time, there were only a few fossils of early man in existence, and even these were subject to much dispute.

While these arguments were raging, one man who became interested in the problem was a young doctor in Holland named Eugene Dubois. It seemed to him that Darwin was right in his speculations about man's evolution, and that it should be possible to find the evidence if one looked in the right place. But, what would be the "right place"? Dubois reasoned that early man, presumably lacking fire, clothes and other necessities, probably preferred to live in a warm climate. Somewhere in the tropics, therefore, would be the place to look. Young Dr. Dubois signed up as health officer and asked to be assigned to the island of Java, then a colony of Holland in the Dutch East Indies, and very definitely in the tropics.

During his workdays, Eugene Dubois conscientiously fulfilled his medical duties. On his days off, however, he shouldered his shovel and went digging in search of prehistoric man. And, unbelievably, almost miraculously, in 1891 Dubois found exactly what he had been looking for. On the bank of the Solo River in Java, near a village named Trinil, he uncovered fragments of an ancient human skeleton. Most exciting and important among his finds were the top of the skull (indicating the shape of head and brain) and a complete thigh bone.

The thigh bone was almost completely modern; if it had come from some human who had just died, no anatomist would have considered it very much out of the ordinary. It indicated, by its size and shape, that the person from whom it came was over five feet in height, and must have stood fully erect. The piece of skull, on the other hand, could not have come from any human of the varieties presently to be found on earth. The skull had heavy bony ridges over the eyes, a very low sloping forehead, and had contained a brain that, given the size of the body, was smaller than any likely to be encountered today. To Dubois the skull was ape-like, but the thighbone was proof that the creature stood erect. Dubois's "erect ape-man" (*Pithecanthropus erectus*) produced a wave of excitement and controversy throughout scientific circles in Europe. Had he really discovered the ape-like creature from which Darwin had speculated that man was descended? Many scholars thought so, but again others disagreed. Perhaps this was simply the skeleton of some unfortunate feeble-minded human with a small brain and a malformed head.

Or, perhaps, there really had been a race of creatures in the past who all looked like this; could they not have been distant relatives of man, ape-like creatures who have since died out? In other words, so this argument went, while the unfortunate and doomed pithecanthropines were shambling through the jungle, the *true* ancestors of humans, elsewhere in the world, were developing the beginnings of human behavior.

It was possible to think of many other explanations for Dubois' find. If Dubois and his supporters believed that *Pithecantropus* was an ancestor of present humans, it was argued, then it was up to them to prove it. As it turned out, Dubois was right, and his opponents were wrong, but their objections were reasonable and their demands for more proof were justified. In science, remember, anyone may offer *any* hypothesis, any explanation for what he has found; but before his ideas can be accepted, more and more evidence must be presented in their support.

In the matter of *Pithecanthropus,* more evidence did turn up. In 1927 Davidson Black, an American anatomist living in China, began to find pieces of ancient human skeletal material in a cave near the town of Chou-kou-tien, not far from the city of Peking. Eventually, a large number of fossil humans were found, along with stone tools and much debris from daily life. Unfortunately, all the fossil material disappeared during the upheaval of the second World War, and has never been found again. Luckily, however, before they were lost the bones were carefully studied by many scientists.

Essentially, they were pithecanthropine in type, very similar to the one found in Java by Dubois, if with slightly larger brains. The Chinese pithecanthropines were younger; that is, they lived closer to the present time. Other similar fossils have been identified in Europe (the so-called Heidelberg Jaw found in Germany) and in Africa, and more were later found in Java.

It is now generally agreed by most anthropologists that by about five hundred thousand to three hundred thousand years ago, man's ancestors had evolved from the earlier australopithecine type into the pithecanthropine type, and were scattered over most of the Old World, Asia, Europe and Africa. By this time, man had achieved pretty much full human size and shape. The head and brain had become much more human-like, but had not yet completed its evolutionary course. By this time, too, there can be no question that man was making many varieties of tools and weapons. There are even different styles to be noted in different parts of the world. In China, at least, he was living in caves, and many believe that he even had the use of fire.

The term Pithecanthropus (ape-man), therefore, is dropping out of use. Most scholars prefer to call man of that period *Homo erectus*, the stage between *Homo africanus* and true *Homo sapiens*, although there are even some who say that the pithecanthropines were so human-like they deserve the name of *Homo sapiens*.

By one hundred and fifty thousand years ago, however, man had evolved to the point that few would today deny him the label *Homo sapiens*, even though he was still slightly different from present varieties until about forty or fifty thousand years ago. One hundred thousand to sixty thousand years ago, man's brain had completed its evolution to full human size. The face took a little longer, and is the only feature that sets him off from present-day man. He definitely had fire, for he was able to survive in Europe during the last ice age, when the climate north of the Mediterranean Sea resembled that of present-day northern Canada. He probably sewed skins together to make clothes to keep him warm, and had a wide variety of tools and weapons, often beautifully crafted.

What is more important is that man's ancestors of fifty or sixty thousand years ago appear to have had religious beliefs and a feeling for "higher things." Professor Ralph Solecki of Columbia University uncovered, in Shanidar Cave in Iraq, fossils dating back sixty thousand years or more. One skeleton of an old man had been given what can only be called a true burial, for the body had been laid to rest upon a deep bed of flowers. In Europe, finds dating from this period appear to indicate the use of animals, particularly bears, in religious ceremonies. Burial with flowers and religious ceremonies are both strong evidence that we are dealing here with humans—in the deepest sense of the word.

Because human faces of the period from about one hundred fifty thousand to about fifty thousand years ago had still not evolved into fully modern appearance, some anthropologists give fossils of that period a different name, and refer to them as *neanderthaloids* after the Neanderthal (nee–an'–der–tall) Valley in Germany where one of the first fossils of this type was found. There is also some argument about whether all the neanderthaloids are ancestral to present man, or whether some represented a deviant line that separated and died out.

What is agreed to by most anthropologists today, however, is that, after the pithecanthropine phase, man's ancestors passed through a neanderthaloid phase just before evolving into his present form. Increasingly, anthropologists therefore consider the neanderthaloids to be *Homo sapiens*—although many prefer to term them *Homo sapiens neanderthalensis* (the *Neanderthal* variety of the *sapiens* species of genus *Homo*). It is agreed by all that, by about forty thousand years ago, if not earlier, all humans on earth could be termed *Homo sapiens sapiens:* the *sapiens* variety of the *sapiens* species of the genus *Homo*.

SOME IMPLICATIONS

Let us review some of the implications, for our study of race, of man's evolutionary history. For fifteen to twenty million years, we have seen, hominids (the human line) have been separate from their nearest relatives, the great apes. It was during this period that hominids evolved into a successful terrestrial (land-dwelling) creature; they were unlike most of their primate relatives who remain for the most part arboreal. This change in habitat led, through the process of natural selection, to certain physical changes that serve to differentiate man from his nearest primate relatives. By two million years ago, if not earlier, man's ancestors had developed feet at the end of their lower limbs, strong legs, upright posture, and larger brains. Though not at all fully human in brain capacity or physical size, and with "ape-like" faces, man's ancestors had, by two million years or so ago, begun to make tools and perhaps in other ways to live in a human-like fashion.

There is some uncertainty as to whether, one or two million years ago, there were more than one species of hominid on earth. But by five hundred thousand years ago there can be little doubt that the genus *Homo* was represented by only one species—tool-making, culture-bearing, and ancestral to modern man—though not yet fully evolved into man's present form. Even by sixty thousand years ago, man's ancestors had not completed their evolutionary development, in physical terms, but their mental capacity had developed to the point where their technical skills, their imagination, and their capacity to express affection seem very similar—perhaps identical—to that of modern man. By forty thousand years ago, mankind belonged to, and has continued to belong to, one single variety of one species.

What, then, are the *races of man?* How different from each other can the races be if for hundreds of thousands—if not millions—of years, man's evolving ancestors constituted the only hominid species on earth?

Further, even when (or if) there were other hominid species around, at any given time the ancestors of contemporary humanity constituted one single species. How can we know that the ancestors of modern man were of only one species? We have seen that even as far back as rampaithecine times, hominids were scattered over a wide area of the world. Then and in later periods, there were many separate breeding isolates of hominids, adapting in different ways to different conditions and environmental pressures. One might therefore suggest the possibility that time and again some group isolated for a long enough time became sufficiently different to constitute a separate species. This is certainly possible, and scholars point to possible candidates from ramapithecine to neanderthaloid. If, however, separate hominid species did develop during the course of human evolution, they became extinct without in any way affecting the human line and its descendants.

As we know, all humans on earth today belong to a *single variety* of one species: therefore, the ancestors of all present humans, at any point in the history of life on earth, however far back, must have constituted one single species. Agreed, at any time there may have been many breeding isolates, with different gene pools. But all men must have belonged to one species because, over all the years, genetic changes originating in one biological isolate or another *spread throughout the species*. With all the local variations, the human species evolved—as a species from ramapithecine, through australopithecine and pithecanthropine and neanderthaloid stages—to our present appearance.

Some scholars, particularly in the nineteenth and early twentieth centuries, used to speculate on the possibility of *parallel evolution,* which is to say that the present races of man evolved side by side, but separately, from earlier types. For example, some have suggested that Chinese and other Asian peoples evolved from the pithecanthropines discovered in China, while the Javanese pithecanthropines gave rise to the peoples living in New Guinea and Australia (before European immigration), and a third type of pithecanthropine (represented by the Heidelberg Jaw) evolved separately into Europeans, and so on. After all, there were biological isolates among the pithecanthropines, and fossils found in one area differ slightly from those from another area.

Perhaps it is possible to imagine such a thing, but in reality it seems to call for too much of a coincidence. After all, the pithecanthropine fossils, particularly the skulls, are all noticeably different

from those of modern men. We are asked to believe, then, that each
isolate, evolving and changing over hundreds of thousands of years
and without genetic interchange, would have descendants in the
modern world who *all* resemble one another much more closely than
any do their pithecanthropine ancestors. Great changes in appearance and structure took place, as we know, yet we would have to
suppose that each separated group evolved in the same way, with
exactly the same genetic changes! Because, even if there were similarities in appearance, if genetic changes causing them were signifi-
cantly different, human groups would no more be able to mate and
have living offspring than can horses and donkeys. And we know that
a human from any part of the world can marry a person from anywhere else in the world and have living, viable children: we are,
after all, one species.

No, such an hypothesis demands too much of coincidence. It is
simpler and more reasonable to assume that, despite local differences
in the separate breeding isolates, genetic interchange took place continually among all the ancestors of present-day humans, and so we all
evolved together, continually sharing the genetic changes that occurred.

Another reason why such an assumption is more acceptable is that
such continual movement and interbreeding of humans seems to be
characteristic of our history as far back as we can trace it. Neanderthaloids in Europe were slightly different from those in Africa, but
the ones found in northern Africa and southwest Asia tend to be
intermediate between the two, just as in the case of the present
populations. When the present variety of *Homo sapiens* first appears
in the fossil record, some forty thousand years ago, there were
different local types (not exactly, perhaps, the same as now) and they
were moving over time from place to place. The first ones to be
identified for what is today Europe very clearly moved into the area
from somewhere else, possibly northern Africa or southwestern Asia.
At that time, and for the next thirty thousand years, the climate of
the earth was much colder than it is at present. As we noted, the
climate of southern Europe at that time resembled the climate of
present northern Canada. The east coast of North America was covered with perpetual snow and ice as far south as where New York
stands today. What is the Sahara Desert today was probably fertile
grassland in those times. During those thirty thousand years, the
fossil and archeological record indicates many movements of different peoples into Europe and into different parts of the world.

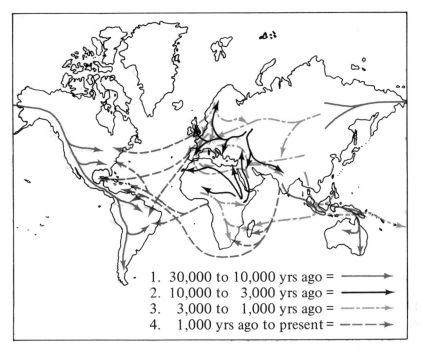

1. 30,000 to 10,000 yrs ago = ———→
2. 10,000 to   3,000 yrs ago = ———→
3.   3,000 to   1,000 yrs ago = — - - -·→
4.   1,000 yrs ago to present = — - - - →

Some of the major human population movements of the past 30,000 years.

About twenty thousand years ago, there was a movement of peoples from southern Asia—from what is today southern India and nearby lands—across the islands that are now called Indonesia and Melanesia and all the way to Australia. Perhaps fifteen thousand years ago, a movement of Siberian peoples across the Bering Strait into Alaska began, and the populating of the New World was underway.

The modern period of the world, and of man, may be said to have begun some ten to twelve thousand years ago. It was at this time that the last ice age came to an end, and the climate of the world began to resemble its present pattern. What did man look like then? Where did he live, and what changes took place during these ten thousand years? These are some of the questions we will try to answer in the next chapter.

13

Human Movement and Variation

Some ten thousand or so years ago, the climate warmed and the world took on the appearance it was to have through modern, recorded history. Human beings, too, appeared in varieties and kinds known to us today. That doesn't mean, of course, that in appearance and distribution mankind of ten thousand years ago was exactly the same as man of today—there were in fact important differences. It means simply that, so far as we know, varieties and types of humans found then were within the range of types still found in the world today.

We have accumulated enough in the way of human remains, from different places in the world, to be sure there were variations, but not enough to be certain of the exact nature of those variations. This is because of both the nature of human variation and the nature of the human remains found so far.

Human beings, we have noted, are all members of one variety of one species. Differences between local types, as you might expect, are even in the most extreme cases *very* slight. And the overwhelming majority of human differences occur from the skin outward! That is, as we have noted from the beginning, human beings differ, for the most part, in the color of the skin, the color and shape of the hair, the color of the eyes, the shape of the skin folds surrounding the eye, and the shape of the nose and lips. But hair and skin and eyes almost

never turn up among human (or animal) remains that are thousands
of years old! What archeologists and anthropologists find—when they
are lucky enough to find anything at all—are a few moldering bits of
bone, the remnants of some human skeleton. No matter how clever
you may be you will not be able to determine the color of a person's
skin from his thighbone, nor the texture and color of his hair from a
bare skull, nor the shape and color of his eyes from an empty eye-
socket.

Carleton Coon, we remember, has argued that man of ten thousand and more years ago was divided into five races: Australoids,
Caucasoids, Mongoloids, Capoids and Congoids. There were, un-
questionably, *skeletal* differences between the populations of various
areas of the world at that time. The population of Europe, for
example, was composed largely of tall, heavy-boned people, remind-
ing us—skeletally—of a type still to be found in Scandinavia and
elsewhere in North Europe. But, ten thousand years ago, were they
also blond and blue-eyed? Perhaps, but we have no way of knowing
for sure. They could have been, for all we know, black-haired, brown-
eyed and tan-skinned. Skeletons of what Coon has called Congoid
types have been found in western Africa, and they resemble the
skeletons of many of the present inhabitants in certain ways. The
skulls, for example, tend, then and now, to be dolichocephalic, or
long-headed. What do we know, however, about the color of their
skins at that time? Perhaps, for all we know, western African skin
color ten thousand years ago was the same as that of the European
population of the time—or lighter!

What, then, can we say about human differences at the end of the
last ice age? Humans varied considerably in size, over the world,
though probably not as much as today. They ranged from averages
under five feet to averages over five feet, but extreme shortness (such
as among Pygmies today) and extreme tallness (group averages over
six feet, as is found in parts of eastern Africa, and a few other places)
were very rare, if they were to be found at all. Humans varied, then
as now, from round-headed to long-headed, but dolichocephaly (long-
headedness) was much more common in the past than it is today.

The population of Europe ten thousand years ago, as we have
already indicated, tended to be somewhat larger and heavier boned
than the populations of northern Africa, the Middle East and eastern
Asia. In general, then as now, populations of tropical areas tended to
be somewhat shorter than populations of colder regions. As for skin
color, the best we can say is that, then as now, most of the people of

the world were various shades of tan. That is, their skins were
capable of becoming darker when exposed to sunlight, and lighter
when not exposed to sunlight. It is likely, though we cannot be
certain, that there were already people in Europe, though we do not
know which ones, who had lost the capacity to tan because of an
absence of melanin in their skin, and that there were people in
Africa who had lost the capacity to tan because of the abundance of
melanin in their skin. Again, we are not sure—if there were such—who
they were and where they lived. As for hair shape, many believe that

At left, eyes with epicanthic fold. Above, eyes without epicanthic fold. *United Nations* and *Japan National Tourist Organization photos.*

the present types, from very curly to completely straight, must have been present by the end of the Ice Age, but we have no way at present of determining the distribution of such types over the world. As for hair *color,* and eye color, we have even less ability to estimate the types present, and their distribution. It is likely that, among some Asian populations, the *epicanthic fold* (an extra fold in the eyelid that causes the eye to appear different—though it is not—from the shape of those without such a fold) was probably present; but we cannot know, again, its distribution over the continent. Finally, it is reasonable to assume that people in colder climates tended to have narrower noses, as they do now, while those in hot climates tended to have broader noses.

It is worth stating again that most of the differences between humans occur on the surface of the body. In a given biological isolate of humans, ten thousand years ago and today, types of genes for internal organs and general body structure are pretty much the same as in any other population. The frequency of such genes, furthermore, is virtually one hundred percent. Types of genes, and genetic frequency, vary between populations for the most part for surface features (skin color, hair shape, *etc.*) only.

Why should there be any variation even in these features? It would seem that variation in gene type and genetic frequency occurs for the most part for body features that are most likely to be affected by climatic or environmental differences. There would be, it would seem obvious, selective pressure for more melanin in the skin among people exposed to a tropical sun. In cloudy, relatively sunless areas such as northern Europe, selective pressure might well go the other way, that is, toward less melanin in the skin, since melanin seems to interfere in some way with the skin's absorption of vitamin D from the sun.

In any case, in all human populations there are differences in genetic frequency for genes determining the amount of melanin in the skin—that is, some individuals are darker, or more able to tan, than others. The gene pools, then, contain many types of genes—in different frequencies—for future generations to draw upon. Further, certain mutations, such as the one resulting in an *albino,* occur in almost every generation in every human population. With such genetic choice available in the gene pool, genetic frequency can be expected to change over the generations wherever and whenever there is selective pressure for adaptation to new or changing conditions.

Let us return to the earth at the end of the last ice age. The population of the world was small in total number—perhaps five or five and one-half million in all—and scattered widely in small bands or groups. A number of groups, in one geographic area, constituted a biological isolate, with its own gene pool and genetic frequencies. Biological isolates therefore differed slightly, in the appearance of their members, from other isolates. Since genetic interchange went on all the time within the total species, however, it is reasonable to suppose that members of two adjacent isolates, say, southern Europe and northern Africa, resembled each other more than did members of populations much farther away in southern Asia, say, or North America.

Now let us begin to move foward in time, in the direction of the present, and see what happened to mankind. To begin with, all humans at that time depended upon wild animals and plants for food. They hunted wild creatures for meat, and gathered wild berries, fruits, seeds and other plants. This being the case, almost all humans at the time must have been wanderers, following and seeking their food. One possible exception may have been those peoples who lived upon fish and other seafood, and who could thus stay in one place for much longer periods of time, gathering fish and shellfish where they were plentiful.

As the earth warmed, animal and plant life changed in response to the new conditions. What had been grassland in Africa and southwest Asia became hotter and dryer, and deserts developed. The human population of such areas decreased, as people wandered away, seeking animal and plant life. They moved into new areas—south into Africa and perhaps north into southern Europe and central Asia. In the New World, the movement of peoples from North America continued and some believe that it was about eight thousand years ago that man first reached the tip of South America. We cannot know all the movements and population shifts, but we do know that man was constantly on the move and that distances of many thousands of miles, in many different directions, were covered many times by many different groups. Under such conditions, we need hardly point out, humans from widely separated areas came into contact. Mating occurred, and genetic interchange took place.

Man Begins to Take Over

Such movements of peoples were of course nothing new. They had been characteristic of man's ancestors for hundreds of thousands, if not millions, of years. But about eight or nine thousand years ago something entirely new did take place. In different places in the world, human groups began to find ways of improving and increasing their food supplies. Instead of wandering out in search of wild plants and animals, they began to domesticate some of them—to raise plants and animals under human protection and care. Southwest Asia is believed to be the first place in the world where this occurred, although the exact location of the area where it all began has not yet been determined. Some scholars believe that the hilly regions of what is today Iraq and Iran was where the first domestication occurred, others argue for what is today southern Turkey, Lebanon, Syria and Israel.

Perhaps one of these areas was where it all began, or perhaps it occurred at about the same time in both areas—or perhaps domestication of animals began in Iraq while domestication of plants began on the eastern coast of the Mediterranean. It is hard to tell, and one of the reasons we cannot be certain is that, once *some* men learned to grow plants and raise animals, *other* men living nearby borrowed the ideas and techniques and started doing it themselves! Wherever it began, therefore, the raising of certain cereal crops (wheat, rye, oats and barley) and the keeping of certain animals (goats, sheep, cows and pigs) spread rapidly over southwest Asia, northern and eastern Africa, southern Europe, and central Asia.

Climate and soil, of course, varied a great deal over such a wide area. Some people found it easier to raise goats, others preferred cows or pigs. Wheat was a popular grain, but rye did better at higher altitudes, on mountainsides for instance, and oats did better in colder climates. Some farmers raised both plants and animals while some found they could do better if they specialized. In the dryer areas, on the edges of deserts, some people wandered with herds of goats or sheep, trading or raiding for agricultural products.

People were continually experimenting, searching for new plants and animals to domesticate which were more suited to their environments. The dog had long since been domesticated (this had happened even before the last ice age ended), but few wanted to eat dog meat. In central Asia, the horse was domesticated, and farther south, the camel. In western Africa, many new plants were domesticated, including millet, watermelon, and many varieties of squash. Scholars argue whether such domestication was independent, or the result of the knowledge that other people, elsewhere, were raising domesticated plants and animals. The argument is an interesting one, but it need not detain us here.

What is important for us is that in western Africa, in many parts of Asia and the central part of the New World—wherever conditions permitted domestication—mankind moved in the direction of raising his own food. In deserts, jungles, arctic regions, and so on, domestication was just not possible.

In some places, people were so isolated from contact they never acquired the techniques of domestication and the varieties of domesticated plants and animals. Australia is often pointed to as an example. It is also true, however, that the original Australians were not only isolated, they were unlucky in the varieties of plants and animals to be found on their continent—for even modern methods have been able to domesticate few if any native Australian plants and animals.

There are two reasons in particular why this development and spread of domestication is important to us. First, wherever domestication came into use, major population changes took place. Hunters and gatherers, as we have seen, must for the most part live in small bands. How large a population can wild rabbits or deer, plus wild berries, support? A field of wheat or rice, on the other hand, or a herd of cows, can support many more people.

With the tremendous increase in food supply made possible by the spread of domestication, the human population also began to increase tremendously. It has been estimated that the population of the earth ten thousand years ago was perhaps five and a half million. Fifteen thousand years earlier, it had been perhaps three and a half million, so that in fifteen thousand years the human population had not even doubled. By six thousand years ago, however (only four thousand years later) the estimated world population was over *eighty-six* million, more than fifteen times as large!

This great population surge, however, did not occur evenly and everywhere in the world. Hunters and gatherers, on the outskirts of the more favored lands, maintained over all this time about the same population density. If there was any increase, it was small and very gradual. The population of Australia, for instance, remained small and quite stable almost up to the nineteenth century.

In the lands where cultivation and domestication were possible, on the other hand, population increased enormously. More than a third of the world's population today lives in India and China; yet at the end of the Ice Age it is unlikely that either of these areas were more thickly populated than any other parts of the earth.

In time it became necessary for peoples from the crowded regions to press outward, seeking less populated areas. From southwestern Asia, buttressed by their herds and crops, groups of people moved eastward into Asia and northward into Europe. The tiny original hunting and gathering populations of the invaded areas were generally swept up and submerged by the hordes of newcomers. Some characteristics of the earlier physical types are still to be found in northern Europe, particularly in islands and peninsulas off the mainland. For the most part, the persons involved represent a minority physical type among peoples who show a much greater resemblance to those of the Mediterranean world. In India, too, the population of the north is similar to that of the Mediterranean.

In Africa, about three thousand years ago, a population expansion emanating from western Africa spread southward, absorbing and replacing the thin hunting and gathering populations of what Coon has called the Capoid race. Groups from western Africa also found their way to eastern Africa, but here they found large numbers of cultivators and herders already settled. There was a mingling of peoples, not a replacement or absorption.

In Asia, the early cultivation of rice, one of the most nutritious of foods, contributed to the enormous populations of southern and eastern Asia. Among the groups most favorably situated during these developments were the *Han people*—the ancestors of the present Chinese. We cannot know how large the ancestral group was when domestication began to be practiced, but today the population of China is over seven hundred million. Domestication in southern and eastern Asia may be as old as—some even suspect, older than—that in southwestern Asia, and this may be a reason for the great populations of the area. In any case, there was much movement of people, partly at least as a result of population pressure and land hunger, northward into Asia and southward into the islands of what is now Indonesia. Here, in Java, Sumatra and the other islands, the pattern we have seen elsewhere was repeated, and small groups of native hunters and gatherers were replaced or swallowed up in the larger number of immigrants. About two thousand years or more ago, Malayo-Polynesian speaking peoples living in these islands began to move outward, seeking new lands. Some moved along the islands and lands to the west, arriving eventually on the island of Madagascar off the east coast of Africa. Others moved eastward, settling on hitherto uninhabited islands from New Zealand to the tiny atolls of Micronesia, to Tahiti; eventually they even crossed the Pacific to the Hawaiian Islands, not far from North America, and to Easter Island, fairly close to South America.

Meanwhile, in the New World—in Mexico, Central America, and the east coast of South America as far south as what is now northern Chile—the domestication of corn, potatoes and many other plants was contributing to a separate population increase. There is much dispute, still, about how many people lived in the New World in the time of Columbus, but there can be no doubt that, however many there were, the overwhelming majority lived in the lands, such as

Mexico and Peru, where cultivation was being practiced. North and south of the New World cultivators there were only small bands of roving hunters and gatherers.

We see, therefore, that whatever the proportions of different human types *before* the development and spread of cultivation, a very different picture emerges in the later period. Carleton Coon has argued that what he has called Australoid and Capoid types represented segments of the total human population roughly equal in number to the other segments. Let us pretend that each of the five types he refers to accounted for a fifth of the human population at the end of the Ice Age. If that were actually so, then each of the five accounted for some one million people. The major population increases, however, took place in western Africa, the lands around the Mediterranean, and eastern and southern Asia. Even if it were true that Capoids and Australoids, as types, comprised a million people each—their numbers would be insignificant in a world of three billion people.

Cattle farmers in Kenya. *Department of Information, Kenya.*

How Do We Measure Intelligence?

The question arises for many of whether the peoples who developed and participated in domestication of plants and animals were not indeed superior in intelligence and possibly in other ways to those who remained hunters and gatherers up to the present time.

It is easy to tell whether one person is taller than another. We put them back to back and compare them. Intelligence is much harder to measure. To begin with, there is no firm agreement as to what the term means. If a European were to find himself alone in the Kalahari Desert of South Africa he would probably soon die of thirst and starvation in an area in which a South African Bushman could live quite comfortably. The Bushman might claim that the European was too stupid to survive. The European would probably retort that it had nothing to do with intelligence: the Bushman had lived in the area all his life and so knew how to find water and food that the European would in his ignorance overlook.

In much the same way, the European might point to his crops and tools, samples of what he calls his civilization, as proof that he is more intelligent than the Bushman. The Bushman might retort that the European never domesticated any plants or animals, but that his ancestors did! Or, maybe, they didn't either, but had the good fortune to be living near people who did, and simply borrowed the

Bushman hunters of South West Africa inspecting their arrows. *South African Information Service.*

techniques from them. The Bushman's ancestors had no such luck, but that hardly makes the descendant of one set of ancestors more intelligent than the descendant of the other set. "Anyhow," the Bushman might go on, "never mind what our ancestors did or didn't do; let's see who can compose a better poem or paint a better picture." But the result would be a standoff. For in the realm of the arts, it is even more difficult to demonstrate that one people is superior to another.

Some scholars are particularly interested in finding out which ancient peoples developed domestication completely independently, and which borrowed the idea from those who had it before them. The question is important, certainly, for our understanding of where and how and why such important developments took place. But the answers, even when obtained, in no way show that one people is superior to another. Throughout human history, any group of people living in an environment in which cultivation or herding were possible, adopted such practices as soon as they learned of them. It was often assumed, for example, that Australian aborigines were too backward to make the transition from hunters and gatherers. Certainly, they showed for the most part little interest in growing wheat or herding sheep. On the other hand, it must be pointed out that they lived in environments in which neither wheat nor sheep could survive, for European immigrants took over the more favorable areas. When, in the nineteenth century, camels were introduced into Australia, many native people took to them with enthusiasm; *this* was an animal that made sense in their environment!

Since such ideas spread so quickly, since so many more people borrowed than discovered domestication, it is more than likely that most of the people in the world today enjoying the benefits of domestication and civilization are descended from borrowers rather than discoverers. And if that is so, how can a group whose ancestors borrowed domestication five thousand years ago be considered more intelligent than a group that borrowed it only a thousand years ago?

All we can say therefore, with any real degree of assurance, is that population increase was associated with the spread of cultivation and domesticated animals, and those peoples who shared in this spread made greater contributions to the world's total population, changing the proportions to be found of different human types.

Apart from this, groups of humans moved about the world, as humans—and hominids—have for hundreds of thousands and even millions of years. They move to different places as new areas become desirable or accessible, and different peoples move at different times. Carleton Coon and others like to consider the year 1500 A.D. a point of change in man's history; arguing, as was noted in an earlier chapter, that after that date there was so much movement of people that the races have gotten mixed.

POPULATION MOVEMENTS ARE AS OLD AS MAN

But we have seen that movement of peoples and genetic interchange are as old as man and probably older. What makes 1500 A.D. so different, then? Only that it marks the entry of European peoples into that movement! Asian, African and Near Eastern peoples have moved over wide areas of the globe since the last ice age. Europeans were subject to some of these invasions, but they themselves moved little from the confines of the European subcontinent. After 1500, however, there began a movement of European peoples to different parts of the world. They came with *their* crops and herds, seeking new land, just as others did before them, and they behaved just like earlier wanderers when they encountered strange folk. Where, as in North America and Australia, they found sparse, scattered bands of hunters and gatherers, they behaved like West Africans in southern Africa: they replaced or engulfed the fewer earlier inhabitants. Where, as in Mexico and Peru, they found large populations of cultivators already established, they behaved like West Africans in eastern Africa: the two populations merged.

But Europeans were not the only people who moved about the world during this period. Millions of people from Africa—particularly western Africa—were brought to the New World because of their agricultural skills. It is sometimes forgotten that the Africans were skilled in agriculture. We have seen that they would hardly have been so desired if they were not; Europeans in the New World could have found plenty of hunters and gatherers nearer than Africa, if they had wished to! The Africans made their contribution to the New World, in the form of techniques of agricultural production, of new crops (such as peanuts and various melons), and of music and art. And, of course, they joined the gene pools of the New World biological isolates that were forming.

Later, hundreds of thousands of people from India and China and elsewhere in Asia were brought to the New World, or came of their own accord. People of Indian ancestry form large elements in the populations of Trinidad, Guyana and other places in North and South America. They make up large segments of the population in the Union of South Africa and the Fiji Islands. It has been estimated that emigration from India in the last quarter of the nineteenth century was greater than from the British Isles!

The Chinese scattered in large numbers not only in the New World but throughout southeastern Asia. Even in heavily populated countries such as Indonesia and Malaysia the descendants of Chinese immigrants make up substantial segments of the population.

In summary, then: over time there are different rates of movement of peoples; different peoples stay put or move out; some remain separate for comparatively long periods of time; among others there is much mixing of hitherto widely separated types. The pattern continues, however, much the same as it has since the days of man's beginnings.

As a result, we continue to be, as we have always been—one variety of one species.

14

One Variety—One Species

By this time you have undoubtedly sat back at least once and said, "But there *are* differences between the races. Anyone with eyes can see that."

"And," your argument may have continued, "if there are differences it should be possible to classify these differences."

But we have seen that attempts in the past to classify them have been largely unsatisfactory. Man does not fall neatly into three, four, or thirty-four races, and in the preceding chapters we have examined some of the many reasons why this is so.

Where does that leave us? After all, if there are differences among men—and we *know* that there are—it certainly should be possible in some way to state clearly and accurately what they are and where they are. Actually it *is* possible to clarify human differences not in just one way, but in many ways.

Now that we are armed with some knowledge of genetics, evolution, and history to help us avoid all the old pitfalls, let us turn to the basic question of this book: what are the *kinds of mankind?*

SINGLE-TRAIT APPROACH

One straightfoward approach to classification would be in terms of a single, easily detectable, physical trait. If such a trait can be associated with the presence or absence of one gene or a few genes we can call our category a *genetic set*. But even if we are not yet certain of the genetic source of the difference we can at least clearly and unmistakably divide people into those with the trait and those without it. That is, we can arrange sets by genotype or phenotype.

For example, we can speak of the set of all blue-eyed people or the set of all people with type A blood. For such genotypic sets, we know something of the genetic basis of the difference. We can also speak of the phenotypic set of all totally bald-headed people or all people over six feet in height. In such cases, the genetic reasons are still somewhat obscure, and we may be including together people with very different genetic structures for what *looks* like the same physical trait.

Such an approach is reasonably accurate—either an individual is blue-eyed, or over six feet—or he is not—and we have isolated a category of humans from others who differ in regard to that particular trait. It may be useful to set up such a category, or set. Often, too, you will see the term *type* used: type A blood, blue-eyed type, etc.

Such categories may be set up in order to seek the answers to any number of questions. What is the distribution of people with a particular physical trait around the world? Is the trait rare in one place but quite common somewhere else? If so, does that give us some clues to the isolation of one population, or of the recent movement of another? Geneticists can concentrate on other questions. Is the trait produced by the presence or absence of one gene, or a combination of genes, or can totally different genes produce what is seemingly the same trait? Are the genes involved dominant or recessive?

Even more interesting, perhaps, is the question of whether the trait confers some advantage or disadvantage upon its owner. It has been suggested, for example, on the basis of recent studies, that people with one blood type are more susceptible to certain diseases than are people with other blood types. Some studies indicate that people with type O blood, at least in Europe, have a much greater chance of contracting stomach ulcers during their lifetimes than people with types A, B, or AB. On the other hand, people with type O seem more resistant to stomach cancer. If these differences actually hold up, after more studies are made, the next question will be: *Why?* What is there about a particular blood type—or the genetic structure producing it—that makes one more or less resistant to a particular disease? If we can answer such a question, it may help us to find better ways of curing or preventing the disease among *all* people.

Another question, related to the one above, is why the trait is widespread in one area and rare in another. Variations in blood type gene frequencies occur among all human groups. If one blood type provides a greater resistance to a particular illness than another, is that why it is more common in one part of the world than another? Does diet, or climate, or whatever, in one place make a particular illness such as ulcers, more of a problem that it is somewhere else? If so, that would create a selective pressure and we would expect the genetic frequency of the trait to be greater.

An interesting example of this problem has to do with the occurrence of an illness called *sickle-cell anemia*. The illness occurs in a number of places in the world, but it is particularly common in Africa, and most particularly in western Africa. It has a genetic base: in a person who exhibits the illness, the gene directing what the shape of his red blood cells shall be has a molecular pattern slightly different from that of people who do not exhibit the illness. The changed molecular pattern of the gene is the result of a small mutation in some distant ancestor that was passed along to future generations.

As a result of this slight genetic difference, the red blood cells of people who have inherited this gene do not assume the fully rounded shape of normal, healthy, red blood cells, but, as shown in the photograph, have a crimped, or sickle-like shape. The effect of this difference in shape is to make the cells less efficient in their most important activity, that of carrying oxygen to all the cells of the body; they can do it, but not as well as normal blood cells. This inefficiency causes the person with the illness to be more tired, and less active, than a healthy person should be, and in severe cases sickle-cell anemia can lead to death.

It is easy to understand, of course, how such a mutation can occur, but it is certainly not a very desirable one. How, then, could such an obviously disadvantageous mutation have spread over so wide an area and achieved any substantial degree of genetic frequency in any human population? Why, rather, having once appeared, did it not tend to diminish in frequency and disappear after a few generations?

That is in fact what must have happened to the sickling gene in most cases when it appeared as a mutation in a human gene pool. The same mutations often occur over and over again within a species. In Africa, the sickling gene—unpleasant though it was—turned out to have a selective advantage!

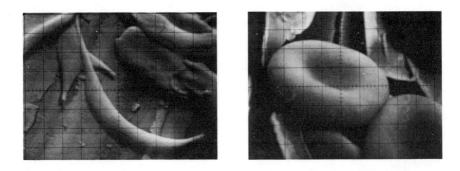

A sickled red blood cell photographed at a magnification of 5,000 times compared to a normal red blood cell below photographed at a magnification of 10,000 times. *The samples are courtesy of Patricia Farnsworth, Ph.D., Barnard College. The micrographs were taken by Irene Piscopo on a Philips EM300 Electron Microscope with Scanning Attachment.*

Throughout the tropical areas of the world malaria has always been a terrible problem for mankind. In recent years, we have discovered that the disease is carried and transmitted by certain varieties of mosquitos. By draining the swamps in which the mosquitos breed, and by other methods, the frequency of the disease has been sharply cut back. We have medicines today to keep people from catching it, and for helping them to recover when they do catch it.

Until the beginning of the present century, however, little was known about how to prevent or cure malaria, and many of those who contracted it, died of it. Europeans, coming as conquerors, traders or missionaries to malaria-infested regions of the world, found that they, particularly, had little resistance to the disease. One stretch of the coast of western Africa, for example, was known during the nineteenth century as the "white man's graveyard" because so many Europeans died there. Malaria was a major cause of their deaths.

Europeans, suffering and dying from malaria in western Africa, noted that while some of the local West Africans would die just as quickly from the disease, many others seemed immune to the disease, or would recover from it if they came down with it. It turned out that most of the people immune or resistant to malaria had some degree of sickle-cell anemia. The organism that causes malaria thrives best among normal red blood cells, and poorly among sickled cells. As a result, the effects of malaria are not as severe for people who have sickle-cell anemia.

An individual, homozygotic for sickle-cell anemia, who has inherited the gene for sickling from both parents, will probably be immune to malaria. The effects of the anemia, however, in such a person will probably be so severe that the person will die young, perhaps in his infancy. On the other hand, a person who has not received a gene for sickling from either parent may succumb to

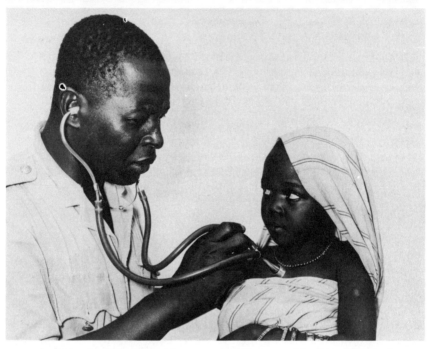

A doctor in Kenya examines a young Kenyan girl. *Department of Information, Kenya.*

malaria at a very early age, so he is not much better off in high malaria areas. But the person who is heterozygotic for sickling (who has received a gene for it from only one parent) is likely to be only mildly affected by the anemia, yet he may still be fairly resistant to malaria. Heterozygosity for sickle-cell anemia, therefore, was of definite selective advantage in high malaria areas, and the genetic frequency for this trait increased.

Today, of course, the trait has almost no selective advantage. It is much more preferable not to have sickle-cell anemia and to depend on medical techniques for the prevention and curing of malaria.

Meanwhile, however, the trait has spread widely in tropical or sub-tropical areas and it will be a long time before it disappears.

This helps us to understand another fact about traits, one we mentioned earlier. They may not have any detectable advantage *now*—as in the case of eye color or hair shape—but their presence in a population is usually an indication that once, sometime in the past, they must have provided their carriers with some kind of advantage.

There is another point we might make. Sickle-cell anemia, a trait caused by a genetic difference, is found particularly in Africa and among people of African descent. Still, it would be inaccurate to call it an African trait, or a characteristic of the Negro race, as some have proposed. In the first place, it is a *human* genetic trait. True, it has a high frequency among some African populations. But it occurs in malaria infested areas elsewhere in the world, such as in parts of India where there is no one of African ancestry. In the second place, even in the areas of its greatest frequency only a minority of people carry the gene. An African, or a person of African descent, who does *not* carry the gene obviously cannot be characterized by it, any more than a homozygotic brown-eyed Norwegian can fairly be characterized as a member of a blue-eyed population just because a lot of his relatives and friends have blue eyes. The *single-trait* approach, which we have been discussing above, is meaningful only for those individuals who have the trait, and they—wherever they may live—are members of the set, but nobody else is.

We see, therefore, that a single-trait approach to classifying people has its uses, but it doesn't help us to classify all the people in an area, especially if the trait has a frequency of anything under one hundred percent.

MULTIPLE-TRAIT APPROACH

If we try to classify populations by combinations of two or more traits, on the other hand, the result is just greater and greater confusion. We know why now, of course, having learned of Gregor Mendel's contributions to genetics. Genes assort themselves independently of one another, Mendel demonstrated, and so we are not surprised to find that traits have different distributions in human populations. Type A blood, for example, has a certain distribution in the world. Its different frequencies in different parts of the world can be mapped and the implications of those differences can be studied. But the distribution of sickle-cell anemia or blond hair is totally different. All we can say is that some people have all three, some have two but not the third, some have one, and some have none. All these differences could be mapped, but the different distributions seem to have nothing to do with one another.

We may note, however, that the genetic frequencies for various traits are fairly similar among populations that are close to one another, and more different among widely separated populations. The original population of Australia, say, before the coming of Europeans, was sufficiently different in traits and frequencies of traits from the population of Scotland, that few people would have had any difficulty distinguishing a native Scotsman from a native Australian. If such differences clearly exist, shouldn't it be possible to draw a clear line separating the two populations? Perhaps—but the problem is where, and how, exactly, to draw the dividing line.

Because adjacent populations tend to resemble each other more than either resemble more distant populations, we say that traits tend to occur in *clines*. This means that as you follow a single trait

A chief of the Stoney Indian tribe of Canada. Originally a part of the Assiniboine tribe, the Stoney Indians now live on reserves in Alberta and Saskatchewan, and also in Montana. *Canadian Government Travel Bureau.*

from population to population the frequency increases or decreases in a fairly steady, continuous pattern. Blonde hair, for instance, is most common in Europe in the north. There is a cline: in Scandinavia, blond hair occurs with the greatest frequency; in Germany and Holland the frequency is somewhat less; in France and Switzerland still less; and in Spain and Italy the frequency is much lower—although blond hair is still to be found in both of those countries.

Given the clinal distribution of traits, and the fact that distribution patterns differ from trait to trait, it is, as we have said, very difficult to draw sharp dividing lines. The population of southern Australia in the eighteenth century was indeed different in trait and frequency from the population of Scotland. The south Australian population, however, was similar in trait and frequency to the population of north Australia, which in turn was only slightly different from the population of New Guinea. The difference was one of frequency, for most people would have difficulty in telling whether a given individual came from Australia or New Guinea. In turn, there were clinal differences—differences in frequency of certain traits—between the people of New Guinea and the people of islands further north, between them and the population of southern India, between them and the population of northern India, between them and the population of southwest Asia, between them and the population of southern Europe, and between them and the population of northern Europe. The genetic frequencies of southern England are clearly different—and yet still quite similar to—the frequencies of the north, in Scotland. And so we have passed along a clinal continuum of populations differing slightly in various genetic frequencies and yet still clearly similar, all the way from southern Australia to Scotland! Where, then, shall we draw our dividing line? Shall we draw more than one? How many?

We could, if we wished, follow similar continua from western Europe to eastern Asia, and (if we consider only the original American Indian populations) across to Alaska and down the New World or back down through central Asia to southwestern Asia to eastern Africa to central Africa to western Africa. Sharp differences show up only where there have been recent movements of people, as in the New World today, or in The Union of South Africa, as a result of which peoples of widely separated geographical areas have been brought together.

Under conditions of continuous slight change from group to group, we can have *no* dividing lines, or as many as we wish. One solution is to try to determine, as best as we can, the number of reasonably distinctive populations in the world. Three anthropologists, Carleton Coon, S. M. Garn, and J. B. Birdsell, have suggested the presence in the world of some thirty such populations—what they have called *microgeographical races*. Some other scholars have argued with the number—proposing thirty-two, or thirty-four, or whatever— but it is at least reasonable to propose that such groups as northern Chinese, northwest Europeans, east Africans, central American Indians and so on represent human biological isolates. The members of such populations tend, after all, to choose their mates for the most part within the isolate and less frequently from other isolates. Such groups, therefore, are worth labeling and studying, as separate entities, because we might learn much from such studies about different genetic frequencies. Sickle-cell anemia, as a genetic phenomenon, may be studied in one individual or even one strand of DNA, but if we want to understand why it has the frequency and distribution it has, we must distinguish a population in which to do such work.

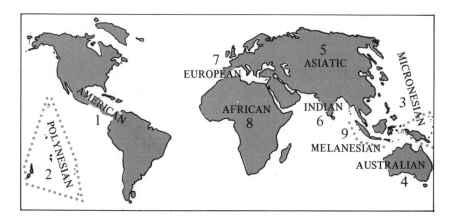

This map shows the nine geographical races as envisioned by the anthropologist S. M. Garn.

A MACROGEOGRAPHIC CLASSIFICATION

Still, we must always bear in mind the fact that a microgeographic population or race is a construct, or fiction. There are subdivisions of each, forming smaller breeding isolates, for example, the British among the Northeast Europeans, and the Welsh as an even smaller sub-isolate among the British.

On the other hand, each of our microgeographic populations is also part of a larger isolate, a *macrogeographic* population: Northeast Europeans and Northwest Europeans are both part of a larger European macrogeographic population. S. M. Garn, the anthropologist, has in fact suggested the presence on earth of nine such macrogeographic populations:

1. *Amerindian*—the total original population of both Americas, before the coming of Europeans and Africans.
2. *Polynesian*—the population of the islands of the eastern Pacific Ocean.
3. *Micronesian*—the population of the islands of Micronesia and part of the western Pacific.
4. *Melanesian-Papuan*—the population of New Guinea, Fiji, and other islands in the western Pacific.
5. *Australian*—the original population of Australia, before the coming of Europeans.
6. *Asiatic*—the population of the large area extending from southeastern Asia, through eastern Asia, into central Asia and Siberia.
7. *Indian*—the population of the sub-continent of India.
8. *European*—the population of Europe, North Africa and southwestern Asia.
9. *African*—the population of Africa south of the Sahara Desert.

Objections and criticisms may be offered for any and all of the foregoing categories, but they should not blind us to the usefulness of what Garn was trying to do. At first glance, these seem to remind us of earlier efforts at broad racial categories or stocks. Nevertheless, it is not the same thing. The very fact that Garn proposes as many as *nine* categories, instead of three or four, is an indication that he is trying to do something very different. These are not useless racial generalizations, but represent an attempt to arrange microgeographic populations into meaningful larger categories. The approach is arbitrary— it is one scholar's opinion—but its arbitrary nature makes it possible for other scholars to question and suggest changes.

For example, one might argue that *Amerindian* is too large a category; it should be broken into two divisions, with the populations of South America arranged in a *South Amerindian* macrogeographic population, and the populations of North America in a *North Amerindian* macrogeographic population. Similarly, some might prefer to put all the *Polynesian* and *Micronesian* populations into one category, and call it the *Pacific* population.

In other words, Garn's approach implies a recognition that macrogeographic populations (or races) are only arbitrary clusters or arrangements of the more meaningful smaller units, the microgeographical populations. It opens the way to fruitful discussion of the reasons for assigning a particular smaller unit to a particular larger unit. What boundaries, for example—geographical, social, or whatever—actually serve to keep groups apart, and which do not?

Garn appears to believe that the Sahara Desert is more of a boundary than the Mediterranean Sea, for he places the North African microgeographical population in the European macrogeographical population rather than in the African cluster. Another scientist, after some study, might prefer to conclude that genetic interchange is greater to the south than to the north, and so change the assignment of the North African population.

Furthermore, boundaries change with time: an ocean is an effective boundary between populations until the advent of ships. What was once a barrier can then be used to bring two widely separated groups into close contact. Mountains, on the other hand, are hardly a boundary to wandering bands of hunters, but they can become a separating, impassable wall to large armies, once nations come into existence.

This leads us to perceive a serious weakness in Garn's approach. His classification, like those of so many before him, is fixed in time. It is, as we can tell by now, a classification of macrogeographic populations as of about 1500 A.D. Since that time, many of his categories have lost their cohesiveness and distinctiveness. With the movement of Europeans and Africans to the New World, for example, it can be argued that two new macrogeographic populations have come into existence. There is a Latin American population, from Mexico through South America, including most of the original Amerindian population as only one element contributing to the new one; and a North American population, made up of the various populations containing European, African, Asian, and Amerindian elements of the mainland United States and Canada, plus Puerto Rico and the Hawaiian Islands.

It is possible, therefore, following Garn's approach, but adding the important element of time, to attempt a classification of macrogeographical populations for any particular century. The reader, if he likes, might like to try it for himself. What, in *your* opinion, are the significant microgeographic populations in the world today? Into what macrogeographic clusters do they seem to arrange themselves?

If you try this, however, you must bear certain things in mind. The larger the population selected for each group, the fewer groups you will have in your list. But the larger the group the more it is a cluster of smaller isolates, and the greater will be the range of physical types included. Hence the more likely the arrangement is to be considered arbitrary by others, and the more subject it will be to rearrangement and classification.

In any case, the identification of a geographical population, small or large, is an indication of a biological breeding isolate at a given point in time. It can provide us with information about genetic interchange and genetic frequency. We can study the effects of population movement—past and present—and we can even try to peer into the future. We can study the inter-relationship of environment and genetic structure, and gain insight into the relationships between disease and genetic structure.

Useful and Useless Questions

Such studies, however, will not provide us with information—however much some may hope they will—about which humans are members of pure and which are of mixed races, and which races are superior and which are inferior. A man may ask any questions he wishes, and seek in any way he can to find answers to them. For the scientist questions like "How high is up?" or "How much does a thought weigh?" have no meaning, and so he does not waste time with them.

Other questions like "How high is the sky?" or "Would a six-foot insect be more powerful than a man?" or "Which are the pure or superior races of man?" sound reasonable, but really they are not. Rather they reflect ignorance on the part of the questioner about certain aspects of nature, as far as science has been able to understand nature. For example, a six-foot insect is a physical impossibility; an insect has no lungs and so couldn't possibly obtain enough oxygen, nor could its spindly legs support it, even if scaled up in proportion to the six-foot size. The scientist, therefore, cannot really answer such questions. He can only begin to explain at length what it is that the questioner obviously doesn't know or doesn't understand—which is why the authors have written this book.

Another question some might want to ask—one that is neither unreasonable nor a result of ignorance—might be: "Which of the macrogeographical populations or races are actually subspecies that will develop in time into new species?" The question is a reasonable one, but studies of all the present types and varieties of mankind will not help to answer it. Perhaps, if we could travel into the future a few hundred thousand years, we would find many distinct hominid species descended from our one present species. If so, how could we possibly predict, on the basis of the present distribution of populations, which ones are going to remain separate long enough for speciation to occur?

Actually, if we were to attempt any kind of prediction on the matter, we should first look back at the entire history of our species. On the basis of such an examination, we can only suspect—if not predict—that our species is *not* going to speciate, at least not in the foreseeable future. Throughout the past few million years, the human species has continually moved about its world; populations separated, but then came together again before speciation could occur. We have evolved, so far, as a single species containing a certain amount of genetic variation. Therefore, it is reasonable to suppose that the future holds the same pattern in store for us. We are likely neither to separate into different species nor to merge into one look-alike homogeneous population, like so many red roses all in a row. If we are to survive, genetic variation in certain traits will probably continue to be important. And if we are to survive as *humans,* we will most probably continue as clusters of ever-moving, ever-changing, ever-separating and ever-mingling humans—populations of one species.

In this chapter we have considered some of the ways we might meaningfully divide up and cluster mankind according to differences and similarities of physical, or genetic, traits. Some who read this, however, might want to protest that—with all of our types and examples—we have never mentioned such groups as Negroes, Jews, or Japanese-Americans. Are they not distinctive groups? Can they not be detected, usually, within larger populations?

Are the Jews simply Europeans like all others? Are we to class Negroes in the United States with Africans or Japanese-Americans with Asians? Remember that many of these so-called types are people who have never seen the continent whose name is given to them. Many of them have some ancestors who never saw Africa and Asia.

These are all perfectly good questions, and we can answer them. In this chapter, however, we have been considering *biological*—genotypical or phenotypical—similarities or differences as reasons for distinguishing types or groups of mankind. There are many other ways, however, of distinguishing humans into groups, but they are not biological, they are *social,* and so they deserve a separate chapter to themselves.

15

Social Divisions of Mankind

Are Europe and Asia one continent or two?

Two, you say? But a continent is defined as one of the main continuous land masses on earth. Where is the physical separation between Asia and Europe?

There is none. The separation is social and political. Europe is recognized as a separate continent largely because of its importance to us as the birthplace of Western culture. In truth it is hardly more than a peninsula jutting westward from Asia.

We have a problem, in dealing with man, whenever we try to see him as an animal like any other. In many ways man *is* an animal and can be looked at, as other life forms usually are, in terms of genetic and biological factors. In addition to his biological nature, however, man has culture—a system of language, beliefs, activities and ways—which serves to make him different from all other creatures on earth. We have seen, for example, that the natural boundaries that affect all other living things—seas, mountains, deserts, and so on—also affect man. That is, they separate group from group, though to a lesser extent. But man also has other boundaries, separating group from group, which derive from his cultural heritage.

Earlier, we imagined an island inhabited by mice, crabs, birds, and other creatures. We said that the mice on such an island constituted a breeding isolate; but, we noted, sometimes a mouse from the island might float safely on a piece of driftwood to another island. In such a case, there would be nothing to prevent our mouse from meeting and mating with a mouse of the new island.

Suppose, however, our island also contained an isolated human population, and one member of it found his way to another island some distance away. He could not, as easily as the mouse, settle down with a new wife and raise children. Genetically, there is nothing to prevent him, of course, but how can he meet and marry a girl when they both speak totally different languages? The people of the second island might even have a law forbidding strangers to settle and marry in their land.

Perhaps they might, in some cases, permit strangers to settle, but our poor wayfarer gets into trouble with the law, and is put in jail, because he isn't properly dressed, or he is seen eating some food that his hosts do not eat. There are a thousand and one ways in which a human stranger in a strange land could get into difficulty that could not happen to any animal or plant form.

Even in the United States there are some rather strange laws on the books. In Gloucester, New Jersey, it is against the law to sleep on the street ($200 fine or 30 days in jail or both). Yet in India and many other parts of the world, sleeping in the streets is common. In Carmel, California it is against the law to climb a tree ($500 or six months or both). And in Seattle, Washington it is against the law to take anything from someone else's garbage can ($500 or six months or both).

Visitors to foreign countries have many other things to worry about. An American who wants to live in or visit Mexico may find that he has many problems because the languages of the two countries are different. A man from northern India who crosses into Pakistan may understand the language perfectly, but he may have difficulty because of religious differences. A girl from the United States may find that in Italy she is asked to cover her head and shoulders before entering a church. In Saudi Arabia or Afghanistan she may feel it advisable to cover her face before venturing out, and in India she may want to cover her legs to the ankles!

There are, then, many ways in which people see themselves as different from others. Once a group is seen as different, whether they consider themselves different, or others consider them to be, they may then be given a name or label, put into a category, and even be considered unsuitable for marriage. Once a group is considered *that* different, people find it hard to believe that the difference is only social; many are convinced the differences must be biological as well.

In this chapter, therefore, let us consider at least a few of the culturally derived reasons for distinguishing and separating groups. We will see some of the groups that have come into existence because such distinctions are made, and perhaps we can achieve a clearer understanding of the social divisions of mankind, as opposed to the biological divisions.

POLITICAL DIVISIONS

Glance at any map and you will see at once the most obvious set of social divisions among mankind. Man has arranged himself into political units. When we think of political divisions, we tend to think immediately of nations. A nation or state is usually a physical segment of the earth's surface: it includes all the land from one boundary to another boundary, and all the people living in the stretch of territory in between. Normally a person becomes a member of the state simply by being born within its boundaries.

There is another type of political organization, however, one that is usually called *tribal*. Here the assumption is that we are dealing not with territory, but with *kinship* or *ancestry*. One becomes a member of the tribe, no matter where he lives, only by being born of someone who is already a member.

In some societies, one or the other principle may be seen to carry more weight; but both are usually present, along with other principles of group membership. Thus, in most states, being born on the territory of that state confers citizenship. There are exceptions, however. Some nations may refuse citizenship to persons born in their territory if their parents came from certain "unacceptable" parts of the world. For many years, in the United States, people born here whose ancestors came from Africa or Asia were denied the full rights of citizenship. In the Union of South Africa, today, the degree of citizenship a baby acquires by being born in that country depends on whether its ancestors came from Europe, India, or Africa. In each case, the child has a different degree of citizenship.

Furthermore, most nations, including our own, will grant citizenship to someone born in a far distant part of the world, if at least one of his parents was a citizen at the time of his birth. We see, therefore, that the principle of *ancestry* is used in determining citizenship in modern states. Indeed, as we shall discover, it is even more important in determining membership in subgroups within the larger states. In the same way, membership through kinship is of great importance among nomadic tribal peoples who follow their herds over hundreds of miles of only vaguely defined territory. Yet they have ways, usually, of incorporating into the tribe such strangers as may come and live among them.

Let us return, however, to a consideration of the formal, territory based nation-state. In an earlier chapter we saw how widespread—indeed, universal—among human beings is the feeling that *we* are better than *they,* the ethnocentric belief that our group, our way of doing things, is the best, the only proper or sensible one in the world. Ethnocentrism, as you might expect, is an important element particularly of *nationalism.* Whether or not it is justified, most people feel that their nation is the best, the most deserving, of all nations in the world. Those who question that are liable to be immediately labeled "traitors."

Given such feelings, which are associated with national identity, it is easy to understand why some scholars might argue that the primary biological breeding isolates among humans are the nations of the world. It is not only that the laws of the country often make it difficult or even impossible for a citizen to bring home a foreign husband or wife, but neighbors, friends, and relatives are also very likely to object to the presence of a foreigner in their midst! "Why couldn't you have married one of your own kind?" is the cry that is likely to be heard on every side.

A man's new wife may be very similar, in genetic terms, to her husband; she may even speak the same language, and profess the same religious beliefs. But—if her husband is an American soldier, and she is an English girl, she may find that she is disliked by his family and friends because they think she is different.

This can happen, as we see, even when the people of two countries consider themselves allies and friends, as in the case of the United States and England. When, instead, the two nations are separated by strong political differences, as for instance between the United States and Soviet Union, or Israel and Egypt, then the number of marriages between citizens of the two countries is likely to be very small indeed.

Language Divisions

Language can be another important factor in the separation of group from group. There are people, of course, who speak a number of languages fluently, or who are willing to make the effort required to learn a new language. For most people in the world, however, who know only their native tongues, the sound of a foreign language is very disturbing, and the person speaking it seems strange and alien. It is immediately obvious that a person speaking a foreign language is an outsider. He is, as the Greeks first put it, a barbarian.

Along with nationalism and religion, language has been a major cause, throughout history, of conflict between peoples. Switzerland is often pointed to as a happy example of a country where people speaking three different languages have been able to live together in peace and friendship, but it represents one of the few examples of such a case. In Canada, there is hostility between French-speaking and English-speaking citizens, and in Belgium between French-speaking Belgians and their fellow Belgians who speak Walloon (a Germanic language). In India, since the nation became independent in 1947, there has been unceasing pressure to change the boundaries of the states to conform to the boundaries of various language groups. More than a dozen distinct languages are officially recognized in India today, and within these there are often a number of mutually unintelligible dialects. Speakers of many of these language groups are seeking separate statehood.

Shall we, therefore, draw up a language map of the world, and consider each language group a kind of biological isolate? Perhaps you smile at this, for what has language to do with biology? There are many, however, who see some kind of connection, and statements have been made, time and again in history, that speakers of English are cold and scheming; speakers of French are passionate and emotional; and speakers of German are dull and plodding, and so on. We have seen that many people in the nineteenth century, in Europe, believed that speakers of Indo-European languages were the originators and carriers of civilization throughout the world and hence were superior. Does this not imply a belief that there is some connection between the language and the genetic structure of the people?

GROUPING BY RELIGION

We have mentioned religion a number of times as a factor separating one group of humans from another. A religion is a set of beliefs about the nature of the universe and of man's place in it, of the purpose of life and the way man should try to live. Along with the set of beliefs there are certain practices, ceremonies and customs. Those who belong to, or accept, a particular religious system are almost always convinced that theirs is the *only right*—or at least the *most right*—of ways.

In many cases, therefore, members of a religious group will not approve of one of their own taking a husband or wife from another such group. Again, sometimes the hostility between the two groups, in matters of religious belief, is so great that bloodshed is more common than marriage. When India achieved its independence, millions died in fights between Indian Hindus and Muslims. For almost a thousand years, there was war across the Mediterranean Sea between Christians and Moslems. For almost two thousand years Jews in Europe suffered at the hands of Christians. The differences in belief between two groups may seem small to others, but the hatred and violence spawned by the differences may be very great. Once Protestant and Roman Catholic Christians slaughtered each other brutally all over Europe, as did Shi'ite and Sunnite Muslims in the Middle East. And for some people—as in northern Ireland today—the hostility remains almost as strong as ever.

Again, shall we map the major religions of the world, and consider them, too, to be "biological" isolates? Is the world of Islam, from western Africa to Malaysia, one great macrogeographical population? There are, in fact, those who have argued that religious beliefs are associated with certain kinds of temperaments and personalities, an indication again of seeming genetic differences which no one has been able to demonstrate, but which many in different lands appear to believe.

In Europe, for example, for most of the past two thousand years, the Jews were looked upon as a separate race—characterized not just by different beliefs and practices, but by different personalities and a kind of inhuman behavior. The wife of one of the authors was stared at long and hard by a classmate when she went to college in the Midwest. The one who was staring finally confessed that she had never seen a Jewish person and had really thought that Jews were different. When pressed she even admitted that she would not have been terribly surprised to have seen horns or a tail!

This was not, for many years in Europe, an uncommon belief. But even among those who would have laughed at this idea, there was widespread belief that all Jews were clever and immoral, that they planned secretly to conquer or destroy the world, and even that they loved to drink human blood and poison wells.

A few serious-minded "scholars" sought to demonstrate that all Jews were characteristically different from other humans in the shapes of their noses or the position of their ears. The Nazis, in the second quarter of this century, believed that "Jewish blood" was

A Jew was required to wear a star on his clothing during the Nazi regime to distinguish him from other people. *Wide World Photos, Inc.*

polluting, and that even people who had one Jewish grandparent should be prevented by law from marrying anyone who was "pure."

The truth, of course, is that among the Jews of Europe, as else-where, there were rich men and poor, beggars and thieves, wise men and fools. What they had in common were their religious beliefs. It is hard to understand how any serious scholars could have believed they were genetically different from the Europeans they lived among.

In spite of the preference of Jews and Christians for marrying within their own groups, considerable genetic interchange took place in Europe over the past two thousand years. Many Jews gave up their religion, converted to Christianity, and disappeared into the larger population. In some places, such as Spain in the fifteenth century, large numbers of Jews were forcibly and unwillingly converted. On the other hand, it also happened that non-Jews converted to Judaism and married into the group.

In these and other ways, then, genetic interchange occurred continually, and it should not surprise us to learn that Jews, in various parts of Europe, resembled—in genetic type and frequency—the people among whom they were living much more than they did Jews of other parts of Europe. Jews in Italy and Greece, like the southern Europeans among whom they lived, tended to be dark and somewhat shorter in height than the population of northern Europe. Jews in Germany and Poland, like the north Europeans around them, tended to have brown and even blond hair, and were taller on the whole than southern Jews.

Racists, however, are interested only in the facts which support what they already believe and ignore the rest. Hence the Nazi racists insisted that Jews were a separate race, biologically distinct from other Europeans. It is interesting, therefore, that they thought it necessary to pass a law requiring Jews to wear a yellow star on their outer clothes so that they could be distinguished!

There are, indeed, so many social or cultural reasons for distinguishing human group from human group that it is difficult to list them all and still keep this chapter within manageable proportions. In complex societies, *social class* or *position* serves to divide the people into groups. In ancient Rome, for example, Roman citizens belonged to different groups, the names of two of which we would translate as *nobles* and *commoners*. You could tell a noble by the purple border along the edge of his robe that only he was permitted to wear. Similarly, in Europe until recent centuries, members of the nobility dressed and behaved in ways that were forbidden to commoners.

As we have seen, the Comte de Gobineau spoke for those who, observing such differences, considered that nobles and commoners belonged to different races. Even today, there are those who feel that the "upper class" constitutes a race apart from the "lower class," and who find it impossible to believe that the differences are not genetic, but solely in environment and upbringing.

It is, in fact, difficult to think of an aspect of human behavior which does not serve, in one society or another, to divide group from group. In India, there are vegetarian communities whose members would never permit their children to marry the children of meat-eaters. In certain parts of Africa, in particular the areas under Portuguese control, the man who owns and wears shoes is considered socially far superior to the man who goes barefoot. In certain European countries it can even happen that a boy and girl whose parents belong to different political parties are unlikely to meet and marry.

Let us now see how this kind of thinking has been applied to the question of race.

16

Biological and Social "Race"

There is one social factor that serves more than any other, in almost all human societies, to separate group from group. This is what we referred to in the last chapter as kinship—the belief that one group is descended from a set of ancestors that is different from those of any other group.

Some readers may be a bit surprised to find ancestry and kinship under discussion as a social reason for dividing humans into separate groups. "Is not ancestry solely a biological factor?" they might ask. After all, we have noted earlier that the different species within a single genus are descended from the same ancestral species; that descendants of a particular biological breeding isolate share in the same ancestral gene pool. How can the term *ancestry* be used for *both* biological and social factors?

The term, however, is indeed used for both, and many people think it means the same thing in both cases. This certainly can be confusing, since the term *ancestry* usually means something very different when used in a human social context, as opposed to a biological context.

Let us try to see the difference. In biological terms all of us, human or animal, have a total set of ancestors. Each individual has two parents, four grandparents, eight great-grandparents, and so on.

Since the number doubles* with every generation, try to figure out how many ancestors you could have had, at maximum, five generations ago, and then ten generations ago. The number, of course, becomes enormous very quickly; yet in biological terms any or all of your ancestors may have contributed to the genetic makeup of their descendant (you) in the present generation. You inherited, as has been known since Mendel's time, exactly half of your genetic constituents from each of your parents. On the other hand, it is impossible to determine exactly how much of your genetic structure has been inherited from each of your grandparents; it could vary from exactly one-quarter from each, all the way to nothing from two grandparents, one on each side. Any combination is possible. Perhaps the color of your eyes was inherited from your two grandmothers, while the color of your brother's or sister's eyes was inherited from your two grandfathers. Biologically, then, to speak of ancestry is to speak of the *total set* of people from whom you got genes, whether you know who they were or not.

Socially, however, to speak of ancestors is to speak of the particular set of people from whom we *claim* descent; who are *recognized* by us and others as our ancestors. Since the total number is so large, so difficult to know or remember, every society has a rule that states that one, or two, or a very few lines are important, while the others are simply ignored. In some societies, only one male line is selected as the true ancestral one; father, father's father, father's father's father, and so on. Does this seem reasonable? That is because this rule which is based on the father's ancestry is quite common among Europeans. There are societies, however, which select as the only line worth remembering, the line that goes from mother to mother's mother, to mother's mother's mother, and so on. Many other variations and combinations can, and do, occur.

"But," a reader may be thinking, "while it is true that for social purposes we do select out only a part of our total biological ancestry, still it *is* a part, and therefore it does constitute a biological group." It may constitute a biological group—but also it may *not*—and socially it usually doesn't matter either way; all that matters, in social terms, is that an individual is *accepted* by others as descended from one group rather than another. It really doesn't matter what the biological facts are!

* Normally, that is, unless cousins marry.

Let us consider some possibilities. A wealthy European man (let us call him Mr. X) has two sons, and leaves his property to his elder son. The elder son, however, has no children, while the younger son has, in time, a son of his own. Time passes. Before dying, the elder son of Mr. X *adopts* a child. The adopted child is therefore the legal heir of Mr. X's property—although there is no genetic relationship between them at all—while the genetic descendant of Mr. X is considered too distantly related, since he is the son of a younger son!

The Iroquois Indians, to take another example, were divided into a number of groups which we call *clans*. A person belonged to the clan of his or her mother, who in turn inherited membership from her mother, and so on. The Iroquois considered all members of one clan to be so closely related that they were forbidden to marry, and husbands and wives had to be chosen from other clans, with children

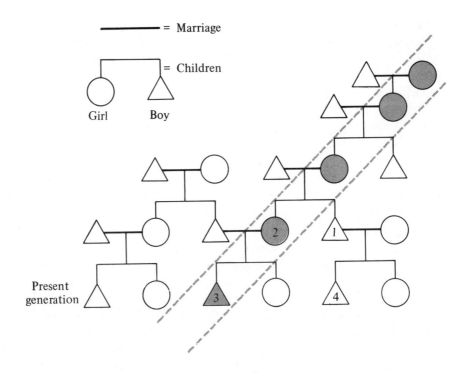

In a matrilineal society, a father (1) would be expected to pass on his wealth to a son (3) of his sister (2) rather than to his own son (4) as we in a patrilineal society would expect. Some of our original American Indian societies, such as the Hopi and Navaho, reckoned descent in this way.

inheriting membership in their mother's clan only. With all the clans continually intermarrying, in this way, it is obvious that from a *biological* point of view the Iroquois constitute one interbreeding population, all members of which receive genes from the same total set of ancestors. The Iroquois, however, would not have agreed; as they saw it, each clan was a distinctive and separate set of close kinsmen; they even believed that the members of one clan differed physically and in terms of personality and interest from all other clans!

Let us not laugh at the Iroquois. In every society, including our own, people sincerely believe that what they define socially as ancestry is in fact the same thing as biological ancestry. In India, for example, most people belong to one or another of what we call *castes* —groups of people who must marry only among their own kind, or be expelled from the group. Many scholars, therefore, in Europe and India, assume that castes are biologically isolated groups, since no one may marry outside the caste and the rule is rigidly enforced everywhere. Nevertheless, as we have seen, when people live close together over long periods of time, genetic interchange will take place. There are castes in southern India, for example, who claim to be descended from immigrants from the north who never intermarried with the local population. Yet they still resemble in physical type and genetic frequency the people among whom they live rather than their relatives to the north!

It must be understood that a social group based upon a principle of common ancestry is very real to the people who belong to it, and to other members of their society, whether we are talking about an Iroquois clan, an Indian caste, or all Englishmen with Norman "blood." The members of such a group "know" they are different, or are considered to be different, and it is necessary to understand such differences if we are to understand the society in which they live. The problem for us is that it is almost impossible to convince the members of any society that what they conceive of as ancestry represents a *social* and not a *biological* category.

Why should we want to convince them of this? Normally there is no sensible reason to disturb or upset such very basic beliefs, to cause people to question the very principles on which their societies are built, to force them to face the fact that they are not really descended from the ancestors who are so important to them. Sometimes, however, the confusion of social principle with biological fact can result in much suffering. Perhaps a statement of the underlying biological reality can diminish some of the suffering. Sometimes, too, scientific research is conducted under the assumption that the social fiction is the biological reality and then much needless confusion can result and the research made worthless. Let us take, as a case in point, that of the so-called "Negro race" in the United States.

THE "NEGRO RACE"

In 1619, a group of men and women were brought from western Africa to Virginia, one of the original colonies in North America settled by Europeans. The Europeans were primarily from the British Isles. Over the following three and one-half centuries, people numbering in the hundreds of thousands, perhaps millions, were brought from Africa to North America. Many millions more came or were brought from Europe. The present population of the United States, then, is composed primarily of people descended from Europeans and Africans.*

Thus the present population of the United States is commonly believed to be composed of two major groups of unequal size. One group, known as the *white race,* is made up of people who have, or who are believed to have, only European ancestors. The second group is called the *Negro* (or *black*) *race* and includes all those with African ancestors. Throughout the history of the United States, various laws and rigid customs have operated to keep to a very low number the number of marriages taking place between the two groups. Some scientists, therefore, interested in studying differences between people—such as intelligence, alcoholism, size of infants at birth, or whatever—have assumed that whites and blacks in the United States constitute two *biologically distinct* groups with whom such studies could be made. Few would deny that the two groups are *socially* separate, just as two Iroquois clans are socially separate. Whether there is a *biological* dividing line between them, however, and where exactly it is located, is a matter of considerable complexity.

In spite of all laws and customs, considerable genetic interchange in both directions has taken place in the United States among people of both African and European descent. In both groups there are

---

* There were also immigrants from Asia and the original Amerindian population, but these made comparatively small countributions to the gene pool. In any case, for this discussion, we want to concentrate on the European and African elements.

large numbers of people who have—*biologically* speaking—both European and African ancestors. It is extremely difficult for many Americans, particularly those who consider themselves white, to believe this, and most of all it is difficult for them to believe that the genetic interchange has gone *both* ways, and that there are large numbers of whites with African ancestors.

It is easier—if still a bit disturbing for some—to recognize that the group called *Negro* includes people with some European ancestry. This is partly because one of the major determinants of ancestry in the United States is skin color. (Who would know—or care—whether another part of the body like a liver or a lung reflected African genetic heritage?) Skin color varies so greatly among American so-called blacks that it is difficult to escape the conclusion that considerable genetic interchange has taken place between blacks and whites.

Another reason, however, that it is easier for Americans to accept the fact that genetic interchange occurred among the ancestors of American blacks but not of American whites derives from the principles in use for defining the two groups. In the United States—popularly, if not always legally—membership in the Negro race is assigned to anyone who is known to have, believed to have, or admits to have—*one* ancestor deriving from Africa south of the Sahara.

It follows, then, that a member of the white race must be someone who has *no* African ancestors! This makes it difficult for many to come to grips with the possibility that there are today among the white population in the United States genes of African derivation.

Even scholars and scientists who are members of the American white race group appear to have difficulty in recognizing that the social definition has little to do with biological reality. Social scientists have pointed out for years something that most people who have been classified as Negroes have always known anyway: over the years, hundreds of thousands of members of the Negro race who could *pass*—that is, who had sufficient European ancestry that their African ancestry would not be easily perceived—simply moved to a different part of the country and stopped identifying themselves as Negro. Some may say that such people hardly mattered, since if they looked as white as that, how much African ancestry could they have? We, of course, know better. Mendel has taught us that genes assort independently, and never merge. A person can "pass" if his skin color genes came from his European rather than his African ancestors. It doesn't matter if the rest of his genes came from his *African* an-cestors. Nor have we any way of perceiving how many of a given white-skinned American's genes are of African derivation.

Suppose that a doctor noted that a particular illness, say, tuber-culosis, was more common among Negro patients than among white ones. The hypothesis might occur to him that there was a genetic difference, that perhaps whites had a genetic trait making them more resistant to the disease. This is a reasonable hypothesis, whether or not it turns out in the end to be correct, and certainly worthy of being investigated; but how shall we study it? Let us suppose we conduct a survey, in a number of hospitals, and find that the doctor's suspicions are correct. (Remember, this is another case where we are just making things up for the sake of illustration.) We find, let us imagine, that 80 percent of the people suffering from tuberculosis, all over the country, are members of the Negro race—while only 20 percent of those with the illness are members of the white race. Doesn't this prove that the hypothesis was correct, that whites and Negroes are genetically different in respect to resistance to the disease?

No, it doesn't. Our samples, to begin with, are genetically so mixed up that we can *suspect* anything, but we can't be *sure* of anything. Most of all, we can't be sure where to draw dividing lines. Maybe, for example, it is true that the original African gene pool lacked genetic resistance to tuberculosis, indicating that the whites with the illness had some African ancestry, at least for this trait. On the other hand, suppose it turns out that the Negroes who are suffering from the illness are genetically more European than the ones who are well? Furthermore, we would want to know exactly which genes are involved, in order to begin to determine whether—in a given *person*—he had European or African genetic structure for that trait. Our statistical findings would not, however, be completely worthless; they indicate a direction for further study. Maybe there are genetic differences, or maybe resistance to the illness turns out to be related to an entirely *non-genetic* factor; where people live, or diet, or something. If, for example, lack of resistance to an illness turns out to be connected with a life of poverty, it would not be surprising if more Negroes suffered from it than whites, since in the United States Negroes tend to be poorer than whites.

Whatever our eventual findings, we can see that the mere presence of *statistical* differences—for anything—between whites and blacks in the United States can never be used as proof of *genetic* differences between the two, for in this country at least they are no longer sufficiently genetically distinct populations. A much more meaningful way to search for genetic differences, which certainly exist for many traits, would be to study widely separated populations, for example, those of Sweden and those of Nigeria. No one would be able to argue, then, that the samples might be genetically similar where they were supposed to be different, and different where they were supposed to be similar! Even in such studies, however, the possibility that environment, and not heredity, was responsible for seeming differences, must always be provided for. Humans, we know, are usually much more alike than they are different.

Perhaps it is now obvious why studies of genetic differences between whites and Negroes range from difficult to impossible in the United States. It is astonishing, however, how frequently the same error is made by seemingly well-trained scientists. They know their subjects—whether medicine, or education, or whatever—very well, but they have no idea that what seem to them perfectly evident biological realities are simply social fictions. It is even difficult for them to realize that another society would have a slightly different social fiction—just as people who reckon descent in the female line cannot believe that people who reckon descent in the male line are really serious.

There are many social fictions, and, the way in which Negro is distinguished from white in the United States is by no means the only one known in the world. In the West Indies, for example, a Negro is someone who is believed to have *only* African ancestors, just as a white is someone who is assumed to have only European ancestors. In between are those who are assigned membership in a third race—that of the *colored.* Elsewhere in the New World, in parts of Brazil, for example, a person who can claim *any* European ancestry —even if most of his ancestors were from Africa—can be considered white. In the Union of South Africa, where members of different races have very different rights and privileges, a great deal of attention is paid to shades of skin color. Children of the same parents may be assigned, on the basis of slightly different skin color, membership in two different races, and therefore be forbidden to associate with one another!

We see, therefore, that within any human population there may be groups distinguished for any number of reasons from other groups. The members of one group may believe themselves to be different from others, or it may be that they are considered different because others claim that they are. There may actually be some biological differences, or people may just be convinced that there are. Such groups may even, to some extent, constitute sub-isolates within the larger population.

There is an important distinction, however, to be made between biological and social groups. As examples of the first we have true genetic categories, such as people with blue eyes, and biological isolates, such as the population of Europe. On the other hand, Jews and Negroes are examples of social categories. Whatever genetic differences do or do not exist, it would be better to avoid confusion by not using biological terms to describe social units. Some scholars, therefore, prefer to call social isolates such as these within a population *ethnic groups,* rather than races. This applies to Negroes and Jews.

It is worth noting, to round out the discussion, that an ethnic group can be viewed as a breeding isolate—as can a nation or the speakers of one language. Any such group, if studied, will be found to have distinctive genetic frequencies. The problem is that the factors causing isolation are of the social, not the physical, type. An ocean is an effective barrier to intermarriage until the introduction of ships and planes. Social barriers, however, as between two groups in the same area, are simply not so effective. This is true regardless of whether they are based on religion, language or presumed ancestry. In time, the social isolates within a larger geographic population come more and more to resemble one another genetically. Any study of differences between two such social isolates, therefore, which attributes the differences to biology is likely to come to grief.

The term *race* has been used, at one time or another, for almost every category discussed in this and the preceding two chapters. You can easily find references in literature, scholarly or otherwise, to the following races:

> The blue-eyed race
> The Mediterranean race
> The European race
> The white race
> The Jewish race
> The Irish race
> The German race
> and on and on . . .

For which, then, shall *we* use the term *race?* For any that we wish to. However, if we want to be really accurate, there are better terms available for all: the *blue-eyed genetic type;* the *Mediterranean microgeographical population;* the *European macrogeographical population;* the *Negro (or Jewish) ethnic group* in the United States; and so on. It is easy to see that there are many kinds of mankind; you will have to decide for yourself how many "races" there are!

17

Why Study Race?

Professor Sherwood Washburn, a noted physical anthropologist, once stated:

> Since races are open systems which are intergrading, the number of races will depend on the purpose of the classification . . . I think we should require people who propose a classification of races to state in the first place why they wish to divide the human species . . .

Classification, in other words, cannot be aimless; it implies certain assumptions about the nature of the things being classified, and the objectives of the person doing the classification. Linnaeus, as we have seen, set out to classify all living things. He assumed, as he started out, that there were in fact significant similarities between species, so that they could meaningfully be classed into genera. Otherwise, why not classify things together for any casual reason that comes into your head? For example, why not simply class together into one group all living things that have hard outsides, such as beetles, armadillos, and trees; and into another all those that are soft, such as caterpillars, birds, and pigs?

Linnaeus, in addition, had no idea that species were genetically related—that species in one genus had evolved from a common ancestral species—and so his classifications have had to be modified since the work of Darwin and Mendel and others.

In the same way, attempts to classify man depend upon the assumptions and ambitions of the classifier. The assumption that there are, or were, pure human groups *will* lead to one kind of classification. But it is one that is unacceptable to those who would base their work on currently held theories of genetics and evolution. For such scholars, the kinds of mankind to be identified (the number of races, if you like) depend upon the interests of the person who wishes to do research on them.

If the interest is in genetic differences, it is necessary to isolate genetic types, as in the case of research into human blood types and their differential responses to certain illnesses. It is vitally important to determine whether or not the differences observed statistically are due to different heredity or to different environment. With traits like eye color or blood type, it is relatively easy to demonstrate that the differences are solely genetic. With traits like intelligence, it sometimes seems impossible to find two scholars who agree on the definition of the trait, or on how to measure it, let alone the degree to which differences are caused by heredity or environment.

There *is* an advantage, on the other hand, in classifying mankind into microgeographic populations to determine differences in genetic frequency and in the availability of certain traits to the gene pool. In this way, we can learn more about human adaptation at different times and under different conditions. We can also chart, in this way, the movement and the isolation of populations over time.

Isolation and genetic interchange can also be studied on a larger canvas, by arranging the microgeographical populations into bigger clusters, or macrogeographical populations. To do this meaningfully, however, we must specify the particular point in time—say, the century—we want to study, for human populations, micro and macro, change greatly in composition over time. Furthermore, when we attempt to visualize man in terms of macrogeographical populations, we must never forget that the micro divisions of such a population are usually more meaningful, in biological terms, than is the larger cluster. The idea of the macrogeographical population is much more of a human construct.

This caution applies even more to any study of ethnic groups, or groups of mankind distinguished from others for what are primarily social, rather than biological, reasons. Such groups are very interesting to study for many reasons. Through such studies, we gain much insight into the basic or common nature of all human societies. We learn about the range of possibilities in ways of life that man has experimented with, and we can begin to perceive the advantages and disadvantages of certain ways, whether those of our own society or of another. If we are concerned about human suffering and unhappiness, it is through studies of human social groups that we may find ways of improving man's lot; we may begin to understand more clearly both the need for change and the ways of achieving changes in human relationships.

One thing, however, that we cannot do when we are studying social divisions of mankind is to offer genetic explanations for the differences we observe. Or, if we do so, we must exercise extreme care.

It is difficult, however, to tell people what they can or cannot do. Shall we tell racists, for example, that they must cease their efforts to demonstrate that *their* people is superior to all other groups? It would be easier to stand with old King Canute on the seashore and try to order the waves to obey. Much better, for us, is to be able to distinguish a racist argument from a scientific one.

That seems to imply, does it not, that there is nothing to be gained from *any* attempt to demonstrate human superiority or inferiority. We don't mean that. People with sickle-cell anemia are demonstrably superior to those without the trait in their ability to resist malaria. Of course, the anemia has its bad aspects, as well. It is, in fact, extremely important to study the implications of genetic differences among humans. European women who migrated to the high Andes, for example, discovered to their sorrow that they could not bear live children in high altitudes. The local Indian population, on the other hand, had achieved over time a successful adaptation to the extreme environment. Much suffering can be avoided by a greater understanding of genetically derived advantages and disadvantages. Suppose it should turn out that there are segments of the human population somewhere, lacking certain basic intellectual capacities. There would be serious social problems, and we would all have to face the implications of those problems.

We would have to be very cautious in accepting such findings, however. It is so tempting, and so easy, to conclude that *our* group is superior to *their* group that we must treat any such findings with more than usual scientific suspicion and demand for further evidence. For one thing, such findings seem to fly in the face of much that we already know. If man had evolved from some pre-human form only a few thousand years ago, as was once believed, it would certainly be understandable that some groups of humans had evolved further than others. But man has been evolving as one species characterized by intelligence, with tools and human-like society, for hundreds of thousands of years—perhaps since australopithecine times, one or two million years ago. Long before man achieved his modern appearance, and his modern varieties, he had fire, religion, clothes, and so much else that we think of as human. And if this was true of our neanderthaloid ancestors of over sixty thousand years ago, it is hard to understand how there could be significant differences in intelligence between any of the present human populations.

Furthermore, the arts of domestication and of what we think of as civilization have been acquired with equal ease by humans all over the planet. Some acquired them earlier, and some later, but this seems more a factor of environment—where they lived, and with whom they were in contact—than innate ability. For a hundred years and more, researchers—both racist and not—have looked into the question of whether or not there are differences in intelligence or ability between groups of humans. Individuals *do* differ; in all populations there are geniuses and imbeciles. But, after all the research, responsible scholars have not seen evidence they can accept of genetic differences between populations in respect to intelligence or ability.

In 1961, the Council of Fellows of the American Anthropological Association passed unanimously a statement to the effect that the members of the association were aware of no evidence that would indicate there was any population that was less capable than any other population of participating fully in a modern complex society.

Note that they didn't say they believed that all races were equal—something that racists often think they said. They said, simply, that they had seen *no convincing evidence of inequality*. It is up to the person who claims inequality to prove it, not the other way around. Anyone may claim that blacks are inferior to whites—or whites to blacks—or Jews to Christians, or whatever, but since *any* claim may be made, it is up to the person who makes the claim to prove it. This has never been done to the satisfaction of the scientific community.

We see, therefore, that while the study of human variation is important, the word *race* itself has caused, and continues to cause, much confusion and trouble. Some have argued, therefore, that we should drop the word entirely, or give it over completely to the racists. Certainly, we don't *need* the term; as we have seen, we have more than enough scientifically acceptable terms, such as *type, set, population* and *ethnic group,* to deal with all the kinds of mankind without using the word *race*.

In a larger sense, however, it really doesn't matter whether or not the term *race* continues to be used in scientific discourse. What does matter is *how* the term—or any other term distinguishing man from man or group from group—is used. We can categorize mankind in order to understand the sources and nature of the differences; or to study variation to understand adaptation; or to seek to improve the human condition for all men in all places. This is the purpose of science, and such studies take their rightful place in the annals of scientific research.

SUGGESTIONS FOR FURTHER READING

BOOKS

Alland, A., Jr., *Evolution and Human Behavior*. New York, Natural History Press, 1967.

Babun, E., *The Varieties of Man: An Introduction to Human Races*. New York, Crowell Collier, 1969.

Barzun, J., *Race: A Study in Superstition*, rev. ed. New York, Harper, 1965.

Boas, F., *Race, Language and Culture*. New York, Macmillan, 1966.

Boyd, W. C., *Genetics and the Races of Man*. Boston, Little, Brown, 1950.

Brace, C. F., and Montague, A., *Man's Evolution: An Introduction to Physical Anthropology*. New York, Macmillan, 1965.

Buettner-Janusch, J., *Origins of Man: Physical Anthropology*. New York, Wiley, 1966.

Clarke, R., *The Diversity of Man*. New York, Roy, 1964.

Cohen, R. C., *The Color of Man*. New York, Random House, 1968.

Coon, C. S., and Hunt, Jr., E. E., *The Living Races of Man*. New York, Knopf, 1965.

———, Garn, S. M., and Birdsell, J. B., *Races: A Study of the Problems of Race Formation in Man*. Springfield, Ill., C. C. Thomas, 1950.

Elkin, A. P., *The Australian Aborigines*. New York, Natural History Press, 1964.

Franklin, J. H., ed., *Color and Race.* Boston, Houghton Mifflin, 1968.

Garn, S. M., *Human Races.* Springfield, Ill., C. C. Thomas, 1961.

Gobineau, A. de, *Inequality of the Human Races.* New York, Fertig, 1967.

Holmberg, A. R., *Nomads of the Long Bow: The Siriono of Eastern Bolivia.* New York, Natural History Press, 1950, 1969.

Hulse, F. S., *The Human Species, An Introduction to Physical Anthropology.* New York, Random House, 1963.

Kroeber, A. L., *Anthropology: Biology and Race.* New York, Harcourt, 1963.

Laughlin, W. S., and Osborne, R. H., eds., *Human Variation and Origins, An Introduction to Human Biology and Evolution, Readings from Scientific American.* San Francisco, W. H. Freeman, 1967.

Leakey, L. S. B., and Goodall, V. M., *Unveiling Man's Origins.* Cambridge, Mass., Schenkman, 1969.

Le Gros Clark, W. E., *Man-Apes or Ape-Men? The Story of Discoveries in Africa.* New York, Holt, 1967.

Mead, M., et al., eds., *Science and the Concept of Race.* New York, Columbia, 1967.

Montague, A., *Race, Science and Man.* Princeton, Van Nostrand, 1963.

Simpson, G. G., *The Meaning of Evolution.* New Haven, Yale, 1967.

Thomas, E. M., *The Harmless People.* New York, Knopf, 1959.

Thompson, E. B., *Africa: Past and Present.* Boston, Houghton Mifflin, 1966.

UNESCO, *Race and Science.* New York, Columbia, 1970.

Vlahos, O., *African Beginnings.* New York, Viking, 1969.

ARTICLES

Dobzhansky, T., "On Diversity and Equality." *Columbia University Forum,* Spring, 1967.

Fox, R., "Chinese Have Bigger Brains Than Whites—Are They Superior?" *New York Times Magazine,* June 30, 1968.

Fried, M., "On Pseudoscientific Studies of Race." *Columbia University Forum,* Spring, 1967.*

Fried, M. H., "A Four-Letter Word That Hurts." *Saturday Review,* October 2, 1965.

   * The two articles marked with asterisks (Fried and Ingle) represent opposing positions and should be read together.

Ingle, D. J., "On Average Biological Differences in Man." *Columbia University Forum,* Spring, 1967.*

Kirkwood, K., "The Persistence of Ethnicity." *Réalités,* July, 1969.

Neary, J., "Jensenism: Variations on a Racial Theme." *Life,* June 12, 1970.

Rokeach, M., and Mezei, L., "Race and Shared Belief as Factors in Social Choice." *Science,* January 14, 1966.

Romer, A. S., "Major Steps in Vertebrate Evolution." *Science,* December 29, 1967.

Rowan, C. T., "How Racists Use 'Science' to Degrade Blacks." *Ebony,* May, 1970.

Simmons, E. L., "The Early Relatives of Man." *Scientific American,* July, 1964.

BOOKLETS

Douglass, J. H., *Racism in America: A Continuing Crisis.* National Conference of Christians and Jews, 1968.

Gillin, J., *Race.* National Conference of Christians and Jews, 1967.

Montague, A., *What We Know about "Race."* Anti-Defamation League of B'nai B'rith, 1958, 1965.

INDEX

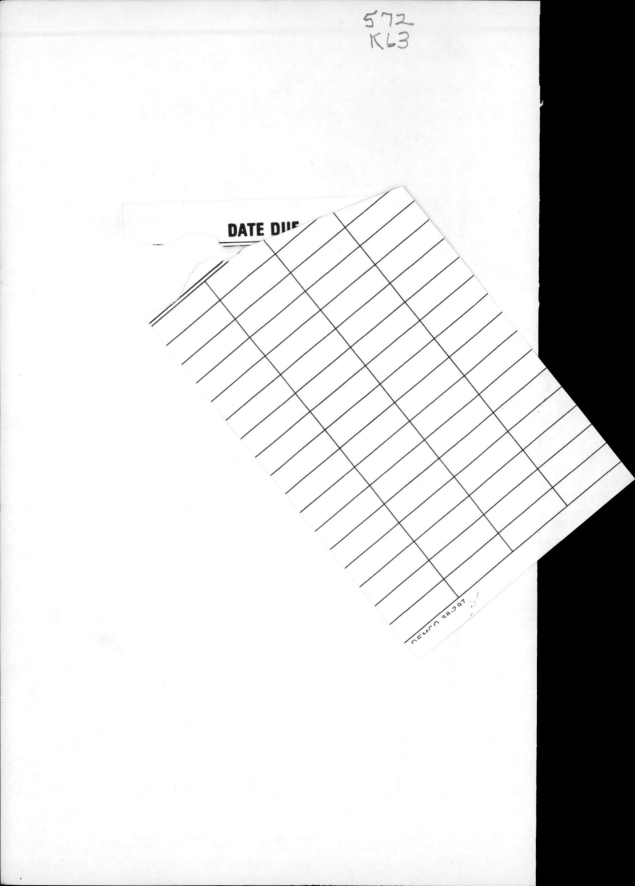

DATE DUE

DEMCO 38-297